FAT GOD, THIN GOD

C 145 529
291

First published in 2002
by Mercier Press
Douglas Village Cork
16 Hume Street Dublin 2
Tel: (01) 661 5299; Fax: (01) 661 8583
E.mail: books@marino.ie

Trade enquiries to CMD Distribution
55a Spruce Avenue
Stillorgan Industrial Park
Blackrock County Dublin
Tel: (01) 294 2560; Fax: (01) 294 2564
E.mail: cmd@columba.ie

© James Kennedy 2002

ISBN 1 85635 398 2

10 9 8 7 6 5 4 3 2 1

A CIP record for this title is available
from the British Library

Set in Goudy

Cover design by Mercier Press
Cover illustration by Mario Parial

Printed in Ireland by ColourBooks,
Baldoyle Industrial Estate, Dublin 13

FAT GOD, THIN GOD

JAMES KENNEDY

MERCIER PRESS

Dedicated to former colleagues, religious men and women, who made unpopular but necessary choices, especially during the seventies and eighties

CONTENTS

With myriad faces, each demanding,
'Why do I not count?'
Enormous crisis kills our understanding,
Need defeats supply.

The Buddha smiles; in him no tears I trace.
Stay with us Christ, we need your crisis face.

From Bernard Thorogood's *Crisis Face*

PROLOGUE

Accounts of life on the missions – those that are available to supporters financing the Catholic missionary movement – are intended to edify. They do not touch the nitty-gritty of personal lives – unless, of course, those lives are in the heroic mould, when accounts become a form of hagiography. The uncertainties, the frustrations, the conflicts, the human flaws exposed by loneliness, disagreement and culture shock, are not on the mission-magazine menu.

The seven years I spent in Philippines – from September 1970 to September 1977 – opened my eyes to that discrepancy, because I had previously worked on the editorial side of *The Far East*, which is the magazine of the Columban Fathers.

Fat God, Thin God is a personal memoir, which goes behind the conventional missionary scene. In no way is it a general statement about missionary life, but there is enough truth in it for many men and women who served in the Third World since the seventies to make a judgement on whether what I've written is over the top – or doesn't go far enough.

I'm telling the truth from my cockpit above the Bermuda Triangle of Columban missionaries, about the years from 1968 to 1978 principally, when 170 of them left the missions to test their mettle as laymen outside the Society, the priesthood, and, for many, outside the Church. I have never read a first-hand account of that kind of odyssey.

There really should be 169 other first-hand accounts to paint a true picture of the exodus, because no two departures are the same. A list of causes is often trotted out: blanket celibacy; disillusionment at the lack of follow-through from Vatican II; hard-line conservatism; Vatican centralisation and so on.

I suspect all these are merely excuses, that the real cause is a shift away from institutional, clericalised Christianity, posing the question of whether we need religion at all!

I could not have written *Fat God, Thin God* without Annette Rowland, who (unknown to me) filed all the letters I wrote to her from Philippines between 1973 and 1977. She was a secondary-school teacher, specialising in Spanish language studies, and a mother of three in Surrey, England. Her husband had left her and divorce proceedings were in the pipeline.

She first contacted me in response to an appeal I had placed in *The Far East* for funds to set up a craft centre and train staff. From that, we went on to become good friends, and in our letters to one another over the next four years, shared ideas and confidences which we were loath to share with anyone else. Our strange relationship, built by pen and paper, freed me to talk to someone, for the first time, about myself and without inhibition.

Although we met in London for the first time in 1975, she didn't tell me she had retained my letters until I had left Philippines for good and had settled down in Ireland. She visited us twice in Ireland, and in 1990, gave the letters to me, because I thought I would put together an account of those years in Philippines, particularly my time in the Zambales municipalities of Subic and Candelaria. The letters became the substance of the account. Because of their immediacy and urgency, I've let them run in their original format, adding chapters and sections only to bridge gaps and flesh out the story. I've omitted my first few letters to Annette, because they're short and prosaic.

The title of the book should really have been *Letters to Annette*, but because the story is about the tensions of life – between a man and his religion, between his old cultural experiences and his new southeast-Asian ones, and between himself and some interesting women he came to know – *Fat God, Thin God* became more appropriate.

1

During the whole of the sixties, J.W. (Joseph William Dooley) and myself lived a lot like country squires. He was a secondary-school teacher – geography, English and religion – and I was an apprentice editor (without hope of succession) and a designer of things, mainly magazine pages. Both of us were parishless Catholic priests in our early thirties, so we spent our off-hours with golf clubs, fly-fishing rods and double-barrelled shotguns, traipsing around County Meath and sometimes even Offaly, where J.W. came from. Our superiors were happy with that. If our minds were concentrated on sport, they couldn't be concentrated on radical post-Vatican II theology, or on women – issues which especially preoccupied bishops and religious superiors during the exciting years of the late sixties, and well into the seventies.

I'm thinking about all that now because it is the month of February, 2002, and I still hate February, just as J.W. and myself hated it almost forty years ago. Then we had different reasons for hating it: the shooting season had finished at the end of January; the fly-fishing didn't begin until March; and we were playing golf on temporary greens, which defeated the whole purpose of golf anyway.

Just as there is a time for sowing and for this, that and the other (*Ecclesiastes* 3, 1–8) there came a time for my golf bag and fishing rod to go into the attic and for my gun to be sold. I'd had enough of them.

Other and less manly things came along for me to do: cultivating bonsai trees, vegetable growing, reading a few books a week and watching sports on TV. And, though my impulse is not to include it in the list, I like a few drinks every evening – either Scotch and soda or a few beers, and sometimes both together.

J.W. has had his own parish now for close to twenty-five years and he's struggling with a serious illness. Our paths have forked too. I couldn't do what J.W. is doing now in his priesthood. Somewhere along the road, I ran out of the faith we shared. It hurts him when he sees evidence of it in me during the all-too-rare times we meet. I try to keep my disillusionment about the Church hidden from him because I know he's uncomfortable with it. From the very beginning he (unlike me) disliked conflict. It was easy to upset him. I remember walking with him from the eighth green to the twelfth in Rosses Point in complete silence because I had upset him. It was the only way I could beat him. Had I let him play his 'cut' wedge over the stream without interference, he'd have stuck his ball to the pin and halved the hole. Both of us played off a nine handicap then. J.W. had a rational analysis of his every shot, to which I listened with only one ear because the more I rationalised my shots the worse they got. My way of playing golf was to walk up to the ball and hit it without thinking. For the first time ever I had hit this long par four in two, my ball jumping over the stream guarding the green. As he was practising his 'cut' wedge I asked him innocently if I should go ahead and hold the flag, which was leaning towards us in the wind. It was enough to take his mind off the job and he fluffed his ball into the stream.

Then I did a very stupid thing: I laughed out loud.

J.W. won the game one-up. The man still has grit on a day-to-day basis. It is enough for me to show true grit perhaps once every ten years.

I have another friend from the old days, another Joe. While I often had to play the crackpot to J.W.'s Cool Hand Luke, I now play Cool Hand Luke to Joe2, who can never be on time and whose fuse blows quite frequently. He likes to describe himself as 'the man from the foot of the Ox Mountains'. While J.W. is five foot seven, Joe2 is a six-foot passionate bear of a man, whose body is always moving and whose mind is always in gear. When he and his wife, Teresa, were setting up their company nearly twenty years ago, after Joe2 left Philippines and the priesthood, we'd meet in pubs and coffee houses before work and during lunch breaks, and I became a friendly adviser for them on things like ads, corporate identity, design of brochures, handouts and so forth. It was all very unofficial because I was working full time for a publishing company, Smurfit Publications. They, unlike the publishing company, never forgot my loyalty to them (even though it was just a brotherhood between one recently marginalised man and another) and when they reached serious money-status, they forgot it less. Which brings me back to the month of February, this month. They invited me to join a golf fourball in Savannah during it, all expenses paid, and while they golfed I could fish. Well, I didn't go, for a variety of reasons. One, I'm not fit and I might be tempted to hit a ball and awaken a hibernating dragon of back pain. Two, I think I want to suffer through the lows of February in Ireland so that I won't dilute the happiness I'm going to feel during the growth months from May to August. Thirdly, and most important of all, it was because of Nassau Street two weeks ago.

She is sitting across from me on the three-seater at the other side of the room. I'm in the armchair with my back to the street, beside the TV. In these positions our greatest conversations and confrontations have occurred.

Since I took the tumble on Nassau Street I have, at sixty-seven point five years, begun to feel the first of my fragilities. I had been tripping between Eason's on O'Connell Street and the other bookshops on Dawson Street like Michael Flatley of *Riverdance*. I was always light on my feet and my agility has saved me time and again from bad spills because, unlike my wife, I am a rusher.

That day, my agility let me down. Rushing across Nassau Street with my hands deep in my overcoat pockets, I mistimed the kerb and head-butted the pavement with my forehead, just above the left eye. When I adverted to my condition there were four well-dressed gentlemen in their forties standing around me. I slowly shook myself to see that everything was in working order and got up. One handed me my cap, the next, my glasses, bent out of shape. The third had found a lens on the footpath and gave it to me. The fourth, who was putting his mobile phone back in his pocket, said, 'Hang on. I've just called an ambulance and it's on its way.'

'I think I'm OK,' I said. 'I thank you very much. You are very kind. And if you wouldn't mind cancelling the ambulance . . .'

And I rushed off. Very embarrassed.

After trying Waterstones first, I got my book in Hodges Figgis. It was *A Short Treatise on the Great Virtues* by André Compte Sponville, a professor of philosophy in the Sorbonne – a worthy book to nearly kill oneself over. It's a secular or non-religious look at the moral values we can and should aspire to. That's where I'm at in my mind now.

'Why didn't you ask the four guys what exactly happened?' she asked. 'You said you mistimed the kerb, but now you're wondering if you had a blackout.'

'I'm 98 per cent sure I slipped. It's the 2 per cent left that bothers me now. It's probably February that's causing the doubt. You know, suddenly I feel an old man. Before the spill, I was just an unfit slob enduring that bastard of a month. Now I'm an unfit old-man slob who just received the first signal.'

'Signal?'

'That my time is running out, my cup is not overflowing any more. When I was brought home by taxi, cleaned the blood off my face and lay on the bed, the room began to go around. When it stopped and I was able to focus again, I began to think some serious thoughts.'

'Such as?'

'If it was a blackout, my time could be limited and I'd go, leaving twenty-five years of my life almost a complete blank.'

'An awful thought, especially for you who can't live with blanks,' she commented. '1952 to 1977, airbrushed out! Imagine that!'

'They were my best years,' I insisted. 'I am proud of them. I was at my best and did my best. And there's no record of them.'

'Imagine that!' she repeated. 'Talking about cups not overflowing, did you have a few drinks in Mulligan's before you dashed across towards Nassau Street?'

'It was midday, Missus. (When I want to be peremptory, I call her 'Missus'.) You know I never drink before six.'

'You often start at three.'

'Only during the short days of February. It helps me to sleep. And I'm usually in bed by eight.' I know from experience when

15

conversation is about to slip into confrontation, so I asked for advice, which is a good way to respond to a woman who is about to give it anyway.

'The trouble with you,' she said, 'is that you are letting yourself vegetate. You're enjoying your retirement, your thrillers, your sport on TV, your drinks with that crowd in Courtney's.'

That crowd? Hold it, Missus, and rephrase.

I don't bite.

'What should I do?'

'Energise yourself. Produce during the dead months.'

'I'd need constant heat in the glasshouse for that.'

'Not vegetables. Produce a book. Write. You did it before when you were in the doldrums. It boosted your ego.'

'You think I need my ego boosted?'

'Yes, that's at the back of all your raving about February and approaching death. You're just after saying twenty-five years of your life have been airbrushed out.'

'No, you said that.'

'Well, there's no record left for your children, family and friends.'

'So?'

'Put it on record.'

'It's passé. Nobody gives a shit now.'

'Not if you use the letters!'

'God, I'd forgotten about them. Where are they anyway?'

'In the same brown envelope they came in twelve years ago.'

By the time I reread my letters of the seventies to Annette, fifteen to twenty years had elapsed since I wrote them – and I scarcely recognised myself in them. They were a shock to me, because up to that day, twelve years ago, when they arrived in the mail with the Surbiton postmark, I believed I hadn't changed much. But I had.

Being a layman had hardened me up and had clipped a lot of the wool off my thinking, especially with regard to women. I was very naive in the old days – an idealist. Almost twenty years, during the eighties and nineties, spent working on women's magazines – *Woman's Way*, *U* and *IT* – tempered both my naivety and my idealism. But what I'm happy to recall about myself in those letters now is how alive and trusting and open-minded I was, and I'm thinking that although I've gained a kind of feet-on-the-ground realism, I've also lost something.

My dreams, perhaps.

The kind of priesthood I exercised then freed me to dream. Later, there was no room, however, for dreams in Smurfit's.

'Did you reread them?' she asked.

'Yes.'

'Well?'

'I cannot and will not paraphrase them as you suggest. They'll have to go in as they are, warts and all.'

'Why?'

'Because you cannot add Fanta as a mixer to good Scotch. If I just pick and choose and paraphrase I lose their rhythm, their urgency, their sense of the seventies. They may be mundane in spots but they are real. And they lead to a dénouement.'

'What's a dénouement?'

'You should have enough French to know that a dé-nouement is a kind of catastrophic conclusion to events.'

17

'Is that what it was?'

'What?'

'Our *affaire d'amour?*'

'Precisely. And, by the way, remind me some time to tell you about Con, the Chivas Regal and the Fanta. For once I got the better of the old bastard.'

'Tell me now.'

'But I'd be jumping ahead four years from where the story begins in Subic.'

'Never mind Subic. I'd like to hear about Candelaria before I made my grand entrance there.'

Since the time the children were small I have always reacted enthusiastically to any request to tell a story and it was an honour indeed to be asked by herself, so I said, 'OK, but you have to let me tell this my own way. I have never been in favour of the news-bulletin format. You know when my sister, Mary Mills, goes home to Brackile for a few days she is able to recount her time there as a story. My father and mother were the same. It was the residue of an ancestral penchant for *scéalaíocht*. It was entertainment. I am the same, although people nowadays seem less willing to be entertained that way.

'Anyway, when I accepted the parish of Candelaria, I had no idea it would be the graveyard of many of my aspirations in Philippines and the end of the road for me as a missionary. No idea whatsoever. You know that now as well as I do.

'After returning to Philippines from a great holiday in Ireland and going through an initial period of angst, I was refreshed, positive, hopeful. And so optimistic that I allowed myself to be persuaded to go to Candelaria out of turn, "for the greater good". I had loved my short spell in Santa Cruz and really wanted to stay there. The sheer diversity of the place, the old Spanish church and the rich agricultural and mining hinterland were magnets for me.

'I fell into that "greater good" trap later in Smurfit's and I know now that when our bosses and leaders quote "the greater good" we're being conned by political expediency. I was a twit then and am still a twit because I tend to trust the boss to do the right thing. If I'm allowed another crack at life through reincarnation, I will insist on one character change: I'll be more hard-boiled.

'The fact that Subic parish was handed over (unknown to me) to two of the young Filipino priests during my absence in Ireland proved what journeymen and transients the Columbans really were. It also showed that continuity of apostolate, especially if it was experimental, doesn't cut much ice with bishops unless they are very rare men indeed.

'In mature recollection, a quarter of a century later, I do believe that the waves Seamus and myself made, both politically and evangelically, precipitated the new Subic arrangements. Seamus, as you know, joined me in Subic during '73, and as well as introducing some progressive thinking to the place, we also put shit in the episcopal fan.

'Enough was enough.

'Candelaria was the next parish south of Santa Cruz, and Con O'Connell, its pastor, being sixty-five, was due to go home to Ireland on a long vacation.

'Con had been expelled from Red China during the general exodus of missionaries in the fifties. While leaving, he caused a stand-off at the border crossing, refusing to leave until a wooden box of books (which he never read) and personal effects, withheld by the Communists in some depot up-country, was allowed to travel with him.

'His co-missionaries, also on the way out, were only too happy to cross over to the freedom of Hong Kong in the rags they wore, but not Con. He hung on, badgered and cajoled until sheer insistence and nuisance-value got the box moving south and over the border with him.

'That was a measure of my friend Con, whom I succeeded in Candelaria and whose wooden box is now out in our shed.

'It was Mick Duffin who inadvertently got me switched there. He was due to succeed Con but teased him that, on takeover, he, Mick, would have to make multiple changes, like scrapping the First Fridays and knocking down a few barrio chapels. (With twelve of his siblings in the US, Con was never short of a dollar, which he spent on new chapels, medicines and handouts.)

'Con didn't see the joke and asked – and then kept asking – the superior, Dick Cannon, that I should succeed him. Nuisance value succeeded. The fact that I disagreed with Con on practically the whole book of mission-work, not to mention theology, didn't make a difference. I was from Limerick and therefore could be trusted. Duffin was only thirty-two and he was an Australian. All Dick – being a superior – and Harry – being a bishop – wanted was that Con should exit Candelaria and not make a scene.

'I surrendered Santa Cruz, therefore, for "the greater good". Con had an unwavering faith and an unwavering methodology as a missionary. He was one of a family of nineteen children from Abbeyfeale, County Limerick. When this fact was communicated to the mandarin as Con was being introduced to his first Chinese parish in the thirties, the mandarin's eyes lit up, he whistled through his teeth and said, through the interpreter: "Your father must be a very rich man? He has many concubines?"

'Not for a second could he contemplate that Con's mother did it all herself.

'At sixty-five, Con had the constitution and durability of a camel. It was said that during an operation in Manila for gallstones when he was in his late fifties the surgeon discovered evidence of a burst appendix in Con's innards. He waited with professional curiosity until Con came out of the anaesthetic and asked him if he had ever suffered unbearable pain and been violently ill during his China days. Con admitted feeling "a fierce oul' twinge, one day, all right."

'He had put his stamp on the quiet, one-horse town of Candelaria. He had the Legion of Mary and the Apostoladas as parish organisations, First Friday communion calls all over the place, a long list of barrio Masses and long rambling sermons in English.

'He invited me to stay with him during his last week there so that I, being a very young man of forty-one, would "get to know the ropes."

'I'll never forget it.

'After living with Seamus in Subic, there couldn't have been a greater contrast of ideas and approach. One example is enough.

'Con had added a bell tower to the chapel in Binabalian, which was only a short distance (say a drive and five iron) from another barrio chapel in Lawis, and a half-mile from the town. While I was with him, he decided that the bell and its tower of cement blocks should have a solemn blessing after the weekly barrio Mass.

'I turned up an hour late. Con was still giving his sermon. Dogs and children were running around. The few men who attended Mass (probably the builders) were at the door having

21

a smoke, waiting as only Filipinos can wait for an event to begin. It gave me time to wonder how Con was going to get the holy water onto the bell, which was metres above him. There was no sign of a ladder.

'Nearly two hours had elapsed before Con, complete in cope and sweating like a horse mowing hay in July, nodded to me to join him at the foot of the tower. He started in Latin and when I realised he was saying the *De Profundis* (Psalm 129, usually said at funerals) I answered like a man. Then he brought out the half-pint plastic holy-water bottle, clasped it, spout facing skywards between the palms of his big hands, and squeezed. A jet of holy water soared upwards, hit the bell and came down in droplets shining in the morning sun.

'Con was in his eighties when he died, having retired to Dalgan Park, Navan. I thought a lot about him on my way down from Dublin to his funeral – mainly his foibles.

'He was almost at the offertory of Sunday Mass in his final parish of Cabangan when he noticed there was no wine in the cruet. Without saying a word he walked off the altar and into the *convento* to get the wine. After fifteen minutes there was no sign of him, and Kevin Farrissey, who had been hearing Confession during the Mass, went to find him. He found Con sitting down reading the Sunday paper in his vestments. Whatever story it was that caught Con's eye in the *Manila Bulletin* not only made him forget about the wine but about his congregation as well.

'Or the time he returned to Candelaria for the fiesta while he was in Cabangan. I knew he expected one of the best Scotches from me, a Limerickman – Chivas Regal, preferably. I also knew that he drank it with Fanta, not with water or soda water like any civilised Christian would. I had no Chivas, but

I had an empty Chivas bottle, so I filled it with a cheap Japanese Suntori. Con poured half a tumbler for himself, added the Fanta and, smacking his lips, said, "Here's to our patron, St Vincent of Candelaria, and to our hurling county, Limerick."

'The last time I met Con in Zambales, you and I were leaving it for good. Con, if you remember, was in his pick-up truck, with his trusty catechist, the middle-aged Miss Tugadi, on the front seat beside him, when I waved him down. Can you recall what happened next?'

'Very clearly. You said, "Watch it Con. Look at what happened to me from carrying girls in the front seat." Con then gave a loud guffaw and released the handbrake. Miss Tugadi had the widest smile at the thought of it.'

'You have a good memory, girl.

'Finally, by the time Con died, there was so much pussyfooting and waffling going on among the Columbans that, to me, the likes of him took on greater stature – for his sheer unwavering convictions and a simple unashamed approach.

'I was in the chapel, alone with Con, ten minutes before his funeral Mass. You didn't come with me to that funeral. The lid of the coffin was off. I looked down at him and said, "Old buddy, I wonder if you've any idea of the complications you caused for me. Rest in peace!"'

'Are you satisfied now?' I asked.

'Yes,' she said. 'It's a great pity you didn't pursue a writing career in the Philippines.'

'I thought about it, but it couldn't happen within a Church framework. Too many *Nihil obstats* and *Imprimaturs* required. You couldn't tell the truth and, at the same time, enjoy being a Columban. They didn't want the whole truth, only part of it

– the good-PR part. I would have had to write edifying stories, and as Peter Hebblethwaite commented somewhere, "Where the desire to edify prevails, there can be no history."

'Anyway, I knew little to write about for the first few years. I was floundering. I knew I'd have to go through the wringer of understanding a people and their culture before putting a pen to paper. Most of my letters to Annette Rowland reflect that wringer.

'It was a real coincidence that she popped up out of the blue and began to ask me straight questions by letter, many of them very personal. Since the questions were floating around in my mind anyway, I attempted to answer them in reply.

'In hindsight, I consider Annette's provoking me into reflecting and writing to be one of the most important services ever done for me. The fact that I didn't know her and didn't have to look her in the eye helped.'

My wife couldn't, of course, resist asking the obvious. 'What about my services?'

A debate on that question would have led me into a series of ambushes, so I avoided it by saying, 'You're with me now. She isn't.'

2

Dear Annette,

Your curiosity about me – and Subic – I find very heartening. As a matter of fact, I love it. My own people in Ireland take it all for granted. I'm a priest in a parish. End of story. There's a logic to their thinking: the Church is universal; the same parish structures exist here as at home; the same training applies whether you're a missionary in Tibet or a curate in Cappamore.

You sense there is more to it than that.

And, of course, there is.

The Spanish Augustinian Recollects built the first church in Subic some time after 1607 and dedicated it to St James the Apostle, known as Santiago Matamoros. By the time the Spanish Dominican friars took over from them in Zambales province in 1679, the church had disappeared. I do not know what happened to it except that it was rebuilt of coral rock under the Dominicans, who cared for the province of Zambales until 1712, when it was returned to the Augustinian Recollects.

When I got here in July 1971, the coral-rock church had been demolished and replaced by what looked like an aircraft hangar by one of my Columban predecessors, Ned McKenna. Ned is good at finance and has a gift for expanding structures, whether they're concrete or institutional, and the bishop is especially pleased with him. As well as building the new church (and, *en passant*, erasing, for structural reasons, the town's major link with Spain), he has expanded the enrolment of St James High School from less than 500 boys and girls to 1,200. I am lousy at structures, concrete and institutional, so it remains to be seen how the bishop will view my performance.

Four miles south of us, on the way to Manila, is one of the biggest US naval bases in the Far East. The local economy is rooted in two items connected with it: employment for between five and ten thousand Filipinos within the base, and the whorehouses and nightclubs on the outside, providing R and R for US servicemen on shore leave. The ten thousand 'hostesses' in the area, made up of amateur and professional prostitutes, make sure the servicemen get more recreation than rest.

Small-scale farming and fishing complete the municipality's economic picture.

On the pastoral side, it has taken me some time to find the direction I'm going in, and now I've settled on two areas of emphasis which are, as yet, little more than aspirational:

1. Family-life programmes of one kind or another – pre-marriage courses, post-marriage encounters, sacraments administered wherever possible in the family unit. Why? Because of the threat to family life by the all-pervasive and loosely regulated sex industry.

2. Crafts and agriculture. Businessmen and politicians

are focused on the quick dollar made from free-spending sailors off visiting carriers. Money that should be invested in local resources – farming, fishing, small industry – goes into bigger and better whorehouses. The quick return on investment! The response of people like yourself to my appeal in *The Far East* means that Rosella and Rolando can now be trained to spearhead the craft project. There is an abundance of raw material in the province for pottery and basketry.

Because the municipality has neglected to develop its own resources, we are easy victims in a food crisis. If the base closes down it will be disastrous, yet nobody seems worried but myself. The Filipino is somewhat unlike his Chinese or Japanese fellow-Asians when it comes to preparing for the rainy day. It's the South Sea islander part of him, perhaps.

Subic town is strung out for a kilometre at each side of the main road, which is asphalted, but has to be resurfaced every year after the downpours and floods of the rainy season. The road is the only one going north through the province of Zambales and south to Bataan.

The houses in Subic peter in, thicken around the bridge of the town proper and then peter out. A feeble, polluted river dribbles from the mountain, down past the *municipio* (the seat of the mayor, his councillors and the police), under the road bridge and disappears, rather than flows, into the sands of Subic Bay, two hundred metres down. The houses are typical of any Philippine town: *sarisari* stores with rusty galvanised roofs and weather-beaten timber fronts dotted with yellow, red and blue signs, advertising soft drinks, medicine and Chinese condiments; the hardware store with goods stacked outside, owned by Chinese; the gas station, which has lines of tricycles and jeepneys queuing up for economy petrol; balustraded private houses – faded relics of Spain – spruced up like old ladies with hedges of red-flowered *gumamela* (hibiscus)and bougainvillea.

Behind all these are more houses, decreasing in respectability the farther back they are from the main road. On reaching the last of them – at the shoreline on one side of the road and at the mountains on the other side – you find the houses are makeshift in both their materials and foundations. Half the population live here in what amounts to mosquito-ridden swamps. They are here because they have no land (in Philippines 10 per cent of the people are supposed to own 90 per cent of the land) and have nowhere else to build. Some will band together and reclaim their patch with landfill. Others will move on.

The swamps weren't here when the Spaniards built the church. Then, Subic was a strategic bottleneck at a point where the Zambales Mountains dipped down sharply to within a kilometre of Subic Bay. The town controlled entry to the province north of it. The mountains were impenetrable jungle, the river, swift-flowing and clean.

Then came the scourge of the equatorial colonies – the nineteenth- and twentieth-century logger who burned, sawed and axed his way through the river's catchment area. He drew away all the hardwoods without as much as planting an *ipilipil* in their place and left the mountains bald and diseased-looking.

Stumps now silhouette the skyline and raw gashes of yellow clay indicate where the earth is slipping away, gouged out by the torrents of every rainy season. With that yearly mudflow, it didn't take long for the river mouth to silt up and for Subic to become a swamp.

About 18,000 people now live in the municipality of Subic. I am their priest.

My last two years have been the most hectic of my life. I was appointed to Subic after a year in language school in Manila. Having spent ten years before that on *The Far East* magazine in Ireland, I had little experience of parish work. I could scarcely give Benediction without making a hames of it. I am also director of the parish high school, St James's, and know little about the Philippine education system. The nuns still run the school and I act as a figurehead, which about sums up my talents in education.

The church isn't finished on the inside – no floor, no seating and, above all, no money. The confidence in me – that of my superiors and the friendly, cooperative people who form a core group in the parish – is, I feel, misplaced. The day-to-day exigencies, the people coming and going, prevent me from concentrating on the solution of any single long-term problem. I am reacting on an ad hoc basis to every request and demand. It is like following suit in a card game.

I will raise money; I will build. At the end of each year, I will leave a trail of baptisms, marriages, deaths, sick calls, blessings in my book. I will go home to Ireland and I will come back and some day I will die, leaving nice buildings and a huge total of administered sacraments behind me.

That is all considered par for the course in this diocese and it's an objective I'm beginning to feel very uncomfortable with. Keep writing. Even though you're at the other end of the world, you are the only one asking questions of me.

Subic, 1 December 1973

Dear Annette,

You do ask the most direct and difficult questions.

Do I feel I have been called by God?

I walked around the *sala*, scratched my head, poured myself a drink and then another . . . And I couldn't say 'yes', because then you'd ask me to explain it. I won't give you platitudes, so here's the truth. This is how it happened.

(I'm on my third gin and tonic here and, like the British in India, we drink nothing less than trebles.)

During my teen years in Brackile, the thought of becoming a priest was never taken seriously by me. It didn't really fit in with our tribal identity. Our crowd – the men, that is – were fond of the women, were more iconoclast than Holy Joe, and very few of them went around seven days a week with shiny nails, soft hands and polished boots.

Then, one day in September 1952, at the age of eighteen, I put on a black suit and black felt hat and set off walking downhill from our thatched house in Brackile to get the bus at Richard's Cross and the Dublin train at Limerick Junction. I was on my way to convert China.

Why I decided to do that – study for the missionary priesthood, that is – I do not know to this day. It was an impulse. Since no impulse happens out of the blue, I've often thought about the factors which triggered this one off. It had nothing to do with holiness, as in saint. I knew little about God or Jesus, and was the worst at catechism in Brackile National School. Nor did I like the long and tedious rituals of the Church. I still don't like ritual, except when it's done with grace and passion.

There were signals, though, that this impulse was not lunacy. I had overheard Katie Walsh Ryan in her black shawl confide to my mother that since the virtues rather than the vices of both families seemed to come together in me, I might 'with the help of God' become a priest like Mother's two brothers, Jim and Harry Lande. I never considered what she would have mapped out for me had I inherited the worst of both families, because whatever Katie knew about the darker side of my family tree, she certainly never confided it to me.

There was another signal, more philosophical in origin.

Out of my father's side of the family there was a belief, often acted out before my eyes, that life could be lived to the full, no matter how restrictive the circumstances. This really meant that we were free to take on any role in life that suited us – poet, plasterer, priest, plumber, thatcher, professor – and that none of them were really any better than the other, despite the pay differential. The important thing was that the job should fit us, not that we should be fitted to the job. There was no such classification as inferior jobs or posh jobs. Jobs were good only insofar as one could extend oneself in them and bad if they became a form of imprisonment. To the old Irish saying, 'You can't make a silk purse out of a sow's ear', my father would probably reply, 'Why even try? What's wrong with a sow's ear?'

By hearing the emphasis put on the primacy of the person and on quality of life, it was clear to me then that it was in the mind and heart that the adventure of living began and, from there, it was kept going. If adventure wasn't inside you, it couldn't happen outside you. Like sex – if it wasn't in the head, it couldn't be in the crotch.

There is a connection between all this and my going down the hill in the black suit in 1952.

It gets me out of the embarrassment of having to say I was called by God. The instant response I made to the suggestion from my cousin Jim, then a sixth-year student of the priesthood in Dalgan Park, that I should join the Maynooth Mission to China was a natural response. It was a job that fitted me.

They didn't know it then, at the mission headquarters in Dalgan Park in 1952, but I had more genuine poverty, chastity and obedience (the major virtues of religious life) in me then, at eighteen, than I ever had afterwards. They weren't divinely inspired virtues then. They were just part of the social framework. I came from ten acres and had a poverty of spirit which St Francis of Assisi couldn't find fault with. I was chaste because my life was totally wrapped up in sports. I was obedient because my father made sure of it.

I suppose going off to Dalgan Park, Navan, to become a missionary in the Far East could have been seen then in some sort of splendid light – a response to a youthful idealism about making the world a better place, intensifying the brotherhood of men and so on. But it had its prosaic side.

It was the solution to an unemployment problem when there was no money for university. And it was, by a long shot, the most respectable form of emigration one could choose.

Outfitted in my new black duds, shortly before leaving home, I looked at myself in the long mirror my mother had in the bedroom. My ears were holding up the black felt hat. My face looked smaller than usual. I barely recognised myself. It was a feeling which took me years to shake off.

Dalgan Park was a surprise.

I hadn't anticipated such a vast limestone fortress, with polished wooden corridors disappearing into the distance. I hadn't anticipated anything, because our circle in Brackile had never penetrated further than the outer wall of the Roman Catholic Church – as far as the sacristy in Nicker – where, with the anxiety of people in a strange environment, they made arrangements for a funeral or paid the priest his Mass stipend for the dead.

There were two highlights to my first year.

I survived thirty consecutive days of silent retreat, which began the month after I arrived. These were the Spiritual Exercises of St Ignatius of Loyola, who had been a mercenary soldier before taking religion seriously and going on to found the Jesuits. His Spiritual Exercises were geared towards conversion from sin and worldliness and towards an intense familiarity with Jesus. He was a Basque. He was also an aristocrat, and ambitious. His spiritual exercises were written from his own personal experiences of conversion. As a mercenary soldier, his job had been to kill, his pastimes to gamble and to sample the fleshpots.

Unlike him, I had little to convert from. Inigo de Loyola (his real name) and myself had little in common.

And so the thirty days of lectures, prayer and self-analysis went mainly over my head. But I survived the course and was allowed through.

Many things went over my head that year. I was already learning how to let them over my head, by practising a kind of eclecticism to ease the conflict between my two cultures – the old, earthy, rural, tribal one of Brackile, which was very strong in me, and the new, pietistic, universal, depersonalised one which I would have to adopt in order to become 'priestly'.

I knew that one day, after ordination to the priesthood, some superior would say to me: 'We have now given you a new image and personality. Go forth and wear them for the glory of God.'

I was too uneducated then to realise the full significance of that.

More than half of my classmates came from boarding schools run by diocesan priests or religious orders. They had a familiarity with – and a cuteness about – the ecclesiastical set-up in Ireland which I hadn't, and could talk about parish priests, bishops and diocesan appointments at the drop of a hat. Some of them loved talking about this stuff, as if they were already in the priesthood.

I kept my ignorance to myself.

I got on well, though. I could compete at all sports, hold up my side of an argument, and had a smidgen of wit. There was a good camaraderie among us, once we learned to cope with one another's accents. I've no recollection of ever experiencing begrudgery, meanness or any form of violence among these men, then or since.

The second highlight of the year was when I returned home to Brackile for a summer vacation in June. The welcome from my family was genuine. I felt, though, that my new role was putting them off. The same looseness or passion of expression wasn't there – as if they had to behave themselves while I was around. They didn't quite know how to handle me. It was as if I had become a stranger among them.

The one unbridled welcome I got was from our terrier, Buddy. He leaped out of his skin with joy, not knowing what wearing black meant. He just smelled me and recognised me.

On returning to Dalgan in September, the one who brought me there, my cousin Jim, gave up his studies for the priesthood after a retreat given by Robert Nash, SJ and left – three months before ordination. He has never told me why.

The following six years as a student in Dalgan were essentially a repeat of one another. No highs. No lows. They could have been extremely interesting years, but they weren't. The most difficult part of the studies to adjust to was the way in which the natural curiosity about life and things I brought with me from Brackile was snuffed out and replaced by a new agenda of questions and answers.

There wasn't even a transition period to bridge the gap between the old rural, tribal culture and the new ecclesiastical one. The new agenda never seemed real to me but I trusted my teachers to know better. I became a product on an assembly line.

Ten years further on, studies for the priesthood became more interesting. Vatican II had intervened and the Church had to make some attempt at gazing at the world around it rather than at its own navel.

When I think of it now I shiver at the sheer waste of it. The only study which came in useful in later life was Scripture. It helped me define a role for myself – priest as social prophet, healer, mediator between people at war with one another, priest as symbol that one can and should always try to transcend the mundane.

The thought of a priest spending a life before the altar, offering sacrifice on behalf of people, was unnerving for me.

During the last four years there, I did something off my own bat which changed the course of my life forever. Since we had a small printing press, I sowed the seed of a college magazine, which came to pass and kept me from dying of boredom. When I should have gone to the missions with my classmates in 1959, I was kept at home as an apprentice to the editor of *The Far East* and, two years later, was sent to the US to do postgraduate studies in journalism.

In retrospect, the seven years of study and preparation could have been crammed into two or three years, and the row of Latin tomes on my oak desk could have been summarised in a few paperbacks in English. After all, we were destined for the Third World, where, for immediate purposes, the penny catechism was more than adequate. It was the total absence of scholarship about other necessary disciplines relevant to mission-country cultures that I miss most now. In practical management terms, it was a dismal performance by both Rome and the Irish Church.

During the seven years in Dalgan we never studied anything about Third World economics, politics, cultures, comparative religions or languages, and we never even knew where we were destined for until the middle of the final year.

It is only becoming clear to me here in Subic why that was so. Dalgan Park aped Maynooth's education system, which turned out priests for Ireland. It really had no option. Rome said it should be so; the Catholic Church was a universal church, using a universal mould to shape universal priests, speaking a universal language, Latin.

In 1968, during a Mission Study Week commemorating fifty years of Columban missionary work, the Society's elected leaders could have raised issues like this, but deliberately chose not to. To do so would have upset Rome and the Irish bishops.

Our two-year philosophy course in Dalgan was only a gesture at the discipline, so far removed was it from the modern world and its thinkers. The search for truth was only an exercise. We already had the truth!

I wasn't the only one who felt I could severely damage my career prospects by expressing any serious doubts in class. Minor doubts were acceptable; they proved you weren't asleep. We were there to absorb and that was it.

In terms of life experience, I was a child then. I was in a bubble.

One has to be living life and speculating about the meaning of existence for philosophy to make sense. Ethics, cosmology, metaphysics, logic, epistemology and psychology make some sort of sense to me now. Then, they didn't. So I handed myself over to the camel drivers and let them get me through the desert. It was the easiest thing to do.

I still think it was the only thing I could have done in order to end up out here.

Some day I hope it will all begin to happen – the drama between me and God.

Maybe it's going to happen now.

PS It has taken me three attempts and three nights to write this, simply because I'm not used to articulating thoughts like these. It has been a therapeutic exercise for me. I find it easy to write to you, because you come across to me in your letters as a woman with a genuine and hard-edged curiosity, and hopefully, in spite of your commitment to Christianity and to our Church, you still hold in reserve some of the openness of your 'pagan' days at Oxford! I think you'll need it.

I look forward to hearing from you.

Every best wish,

Jim

3

It's Ash Wednesday as I write this, and tomorrow is St Valentine's Day. I've no intention of celebrating either of them. She will probably give me a hint about Valentine's for the hell of it but she knows me by now. I don't celebrate anything in February. Nothing. I try to survive. Working with the letters is a distraction, but so far I don't feel my ego being boosted.

I planted rhubarb stools today because there's a touch of spring in the air. I do believe, though, that having had a very mild winter we are going to get hammered by frost and snow before March is out. It will give me time to finish with this 'ego-boosting' exercise before I put on my strong boots and old britches and do some real work with the spade.

St Valentine's Day reminds me of Alice, who takes up some space in the letters, and because of that I'll have to set the record straight. She is now sixty-five and I've met her in the recent past, years after the dénouement, when tempers had cooled down. She is not yet retired, is still a nun and is doing a good job, I'm told.

I first met her in the late sixties. She was a teaching nun in a convent school in the north midlands. I used to say Mass in her convent once in a while, and as often as not she took the sacristy duty. She had charm and style. She didn't walk like a nun or a farmer's wife, but purposefully and with poise, like a fashion model. One felt warmed and revived in her presence. She was a kind of gentle earth mother who had room for everyone. She dragged you into the whirlwind of what she was doing without show-womanship or goody-goodiness.

In the beginning I thought it was all a game, that she was role-playing Miss Jean Brodie. She had vows of poverty, chastity and obedience like the rest of us, but made no bones about them like some nuns did – the moaning nuns. The virtues rested naturally within her person. She wasn't into building empires or monuments to herself or the Church. The only empires worth a *tráithnín* to her were the pure empires of mind and heart. She saw those virtues, particularly obedience, for the practical and sometimes doubtful things they were – in much the same way as she saw loyalty, competence and cleanliness.

Then, for some strange reason, she allowed me to see another side of her. That was one morning in 1968. She looked pale and drawn.

'You look down today,' I said.

'You don't know much about women, do you, Jim?'

'Not a lot,' I answered. 'It's probably a bit late to learn now.'

There was a faint smile at that.

'I had a vision this morning of what I'm going to be like at seventy-five,' she said. 'I watched the old nuns coming down from Communion and, God forgive me, all I saw were wrinkled, self-centred old ladies with the joy of living gone out of them.' Her lips trembled. The next thing, I had my arms around her and she was crying.

She pulled herself away, saying, 'Sorry about that. Mary Jane is around the corner.'

'Who's Mary Jane,' I whispered, looking behind me.

'My period, you eejit.'

During the two and a half years before I left for the

Philippines, we had become great friends. In hindsight these were great, learning, carefree years played out against the background of the greatest public scrutiny the Church ever had to endure.

Even *The New Yorker* in its regular 'Letter from the Vatican' carried insider coverage of Vatican II which was extensive, accurate and readable. My generation thought there was a new dawn coming, that the gap between folk religion (which is what the religion of the people is) on the one hand and Vatican-speak, theologian-speak on the other would close, and we would all end up going the one way and speaking the one language. The Church had to make sense in a secular world or become irrelevant. It was hierarchical and patriarchal and had no mechanism in it to react to the changes coming one after another in that secular world.

There were new concepts we were becoming familiar with: the hope that priests would live the gospel rather than carry on as conventional churchmen doing about ten hours of real work a week with soft, white hands; the redefinition of authority in the Church by McKenzie which based it on competence and leadership rather than hierarchical appointment; the emergence of dissent which crept into the Church from the streets of Paris and anti-Vietnam War protests. We hoped it would become part of church furniture as it had become in secular life – priests and nuns and brothers were beginning to be educated rather than brainwashed. Shelters were taken down and the same educational stimuli which spurred the young secular generation also spurred seminarians and novices – the importance of one's own personal identity and humanity, arising from an acceptance of Carl Roger's psychology, which was popularised within the Church by the likes of Eugene Kennedy.

Priests, nuns, brothers were no longer ciphers in a bureaucracy. They were human beings and personal integrity counted more than craw-thumping. It was even human to fall in love as a celibate, which meant, I thought, there were no marks deducted unless you tore the clothes off one another and had sex.

I had little experience of love up to then but the two and a half years when Alice and myself enjoyed a very exclusive friendship was as near as be damned to it. It was part exploratory of our growth together in this new Church. But it was also hugely sexual in undertone.

In hindsight it was madness to think that a man and a woman who are very fond of one another and who are at their peak physically can have a 'normal' relationship over a sustained period without giving in to the impulse to leap into bed and do what comes naturally.

We had resisted it so far. We hadn't even asked one another the sixty-four-thousand-dollar question: what do you really want from me, apart from having your hand held now and again, and what do I really want of you?

We floated on.

I have adverted to something about the letters which didn't dawn on me until I had read them through twice. Each of them is a response to something the other wrote. They are a reasonably accurate reflection of my thoughts and feelings and frustrations at that time – internal-forum stuff, though. Huge chunks of my experience in Subic and Candelaria went unreported to Annette. I didn't have the time. Then our letters became more and more personal and reactive.

I'll have to remedy that now. I have to create a balance between my personal correspondence focussed on one woman on the one side and a feature-writing approach to the highlights of mission life on the other.

Names and events are clearly flashing to me now from memory, each of which is a story in itself – Conrado, Doc, Connie Jose, the funeral of Mrs Juico, Matamoros, the arrival of Seamus and the daddy of them all, the trouble at Dulo Calapandayan.

I will have to write about it all, or people will think this former parish priest of Subic did nothing all day but write letters to women.

Conrado Custodio came with the job and, like myself, didn't get paid. He was a kind of fiscal, who volunteered his services to Subic parish because he had retired from the US base in Olongapo and I needed someone to show me the ropes and to keep an eye on the business side of things, particularly the parish accounts.

I had heard our twenty-year men talk about the Filipinos' respect for the dead and how the cemetery became a place not of mourning but of celebration – a picnic ground, really – on All Souls' Day. I had heard some of them boast about a marathon of stamina-sapping blessings in surplice and stole under the blazing sun and then, on 2 November 1971, I was in the middle of it myself. That was when Conrado first showed his mettle.

At the outset I thought I would do the prayers for each family's dead at a leisurely pace, taking time for a greeting and short conversation. I was new and most of the people had never met me before. Conrado, however, put a stop to that.

'If you continue as you're going, Father, we'll be still here at midnight.'

'What's wrong with that?' I asked. 'At least the sun will have gone down, and all the candles will give us enough light.'

'But many of the people will be gone,' he said, taking a canvas bag from behind his back and patting it. 'It won't be so good for accounts receivable.'

It was the first time I had noticed the bag and I asked him what was in it.

'Contributions,' he said.

'Jesus Christ,' I said to myself. Then, to Conrado, 'Do you mean to say, when I've finished the blessing, you collect money for it after I've moved on to the next one?'

'Of course,' he said. 'That way I won't interfere with your prayers.'

'Forget the prayers for the moment, Conrado.'

'It is our custom, Father. The people expect it and it makes them feel good to part with pesos for their dead.'

'How much do you charge?' I asked in a whisper.

'Five pesos minimum,' he said. 'But if I see people who I know are poor, I let them off with one peso or even less. We are all God's children, you know.'

'How magnanimous.'

I then decided to fly through the whole proceedings. My mouth was parched from rattling off the prayers in the Ritual and my white linen cassock was soaked in perspiration. Some time in the evening, with Conrado still behind, I came to the last few blessings and to the burial plot of John O'Brien.

I had no idea he had been buried in Subic. Johno, as we called him, was in the class ahead of me in Dalgan Park and came from east Limerick, like myself. We had gone on holidays together once. He was killed in a collision between his scooter and a US Navy truck outside Olongapo. I had taken his simple

44

effects – a box of books and personal knick-knacks – from Dalgan to his widowed mother in Bohermore, County Limerick after someone brought them home from Philippines. Johno was twenty-eight when he died. It was Mrs Soledad who kept his grave clean and who brought it to my attention.

When Conrado and I returned to the *convento* he insisted we count the takings.

'Next year, Conrado,' I said, 'we're going to change this All Souls circus.'

'What do you mean, Father?'

'I will never again traipse around a cemetery for hours jabbering Latin and with you behind me collecting money. Instead I will have a solemn, sung Mass with one set of prayers for all the dead. I will even sprinkle holy water from a platform I intend to build for the altar. It will give dignity and solemnity to the occasion. You wait and see. The people will like it.'

'But what about accounts receivable?'

'Bugger accounts receivable.'

The following year I prepared the people for what was going to happen for two Sundays before All Souls, and on that morning at eleven I was proud of the altar raised on a platform which rested on the above-ground tombs (*nichos*) of two of Subic's families. The outdoor sound system worked perfectly for a change, the cemetery was packed, the choir did its job as usual and I pulled out all the stops in my sermon about the dead.

'Now,' I said to Conrado after the hour-long ceremony was over. 'Wasn't that great.'

'Can I have a word with you in private?' he asked. I nodded.

'I know you don't want to bless individual *nichos* but this woman is the owner of one of the tombs our altar has been

45

resting on and she would consider it a great favour if you would give it a little blessing on its own. It would be a way of saying thanks to her.'

I did it, briefly and furtively. The owner of the second tomb was nearby and I couldn't refuse her the same privilege. Someone saw me do that and there was another request . . . and another . . .

I was trapped, and there was no way out of it.

Five hours later, as the sun was about to go down, I was still there, traipsing up and down, mouth parched, drenched in sweat and Conrado behind me with the canvas bag.

'Where the hell did he get it, did he bring it with him, did he know what was going to happen?' I asked myself and looked at Conrado. He tried to look apologetic but couldn't conceal the satisfaction on his face at a tricky job, well done.

Accounts receivable were on the rails again.

But I knew I had been outfoxed. In spite of the fact that I disliked the mumbo-jumbo of rushed prayers and the raw commercialism of Conrado's canvas bag, I appreciated Filipinos standing up for their customs without need of confrontation and with unusually subtle public-relations skills.

The parish merry-go-round eventually laid me low. Dehydration hospitalised me. I, being Irish, had never been dehydrated before. Health-care and culture studies weren't part of the Columban initiation to the job. It was assumed one would pick things up as one went along.

It was not acknowledged that there was a special challenge in being a missionary in the tropics. It was regarded as much like being at home, except that you had to work through a new language, had to make do with fewer perks and in temperatures between seventy-five and a hundred degrees Fahrenheit and, above all, do it within a cultural framework which you were totally ignorant of. The Filipinos are nice people and it was assumed that if you were also a nice guy, things would somehow work out.

While I was on the drip for my dehydration in Singian Clinic, Manila, I received a telegram from my mother in Ireland which read: 'Dad died peacefully today'.

I waited for myself to react, for shock to set in. A silence pervaded my brain. I didn't hear the traffic outside, nor the clock ticking. The tape of my mind, recording signals and emitting them, was wiped clean. Except for one big numbing message: he is dead.

I remembered him as I left him in the autumn of 1970. He was sitting at the open hearth on the chair beside the blower, a big man in his seventies, enfeebled by a stroke. His waistcoat was shiny with dribbles of spilt tea and soup, because his lip, as well as one hand, had become incapacitated. He wouldn't allow my mother to wash the waistcoat. I dreaded saying goodbye. In the end I just grabbed his good hand and muttered 'Good luck' as if I was only going to Oola. We had studiously avoided revealing ourselves to one another all our lives and it was too late now. My mother, however, took the initiative and I hugged her, saying, as bravely as I could, 'Goodbye. See you in seven years.'

Then I quickly jumped into a Mini I had borrowed, and couldn't hold back the tears all the way to Cashel, on the road from Brackile to Dublin and on, to the Philippines.

I knew I would never see him again. I hoped I would see her.

So here it was; my first confrontation with death at close, family quarters. The fact that I was a priest didn't make me feel any different, nor make me view the loss any differently. That there was nobody with me made it eerie.

By the following day it was still very strange, even though the Columbans rallied round with messages of sympathy and offers of prayers and Masses. It was all about Paddy Kennedy's next life, and it had no immediate impact on me. That I was his eldest son and I was ten thousand miles away during the last big ritual of his life did have impact. I had calculated the time differences and knew exactly what was happening when and where at home.

Then an elderly Good Shepherd nun, in for repairs like myself, struck up a conversation with me. She had a fascinating life story as a foreign missionary, which I had to draw out of her. Like many Irishwomen whose lives have gone unsung, she left Ireland at fourteen, spent years in China and the Far East and was now retired in Manila after a long and brilliant career.

'Where did you come from in Ireland?' I asked.

'A place you never have heard of. Buffanokay, up in the hills behind Cappamore, in County Limerick.'

'What would your family name be?'

'Holmes,' she said.

'Anything to Dinny, the butcher from Oola who has a stall in Pallas?'

'He's my younger brother,' she said, her eyes widening.

I looked at my watch. It was 9 PM (1 PM Irish time) on 27 May 1971.

'Do you know, Sister,' I said, 'my father is being buried this minute in the graveyard in Oola.'

And I cried for the first time.

I found it discomfiting that I got little solace from the High

48

Mass with Archbishop Paddy Cronin, an Offaly man, which followed next day. The words about eternal rest and being home with God didn't quite fit my father and didn't penetrate to me, although the kindness and sympathy of my fellow missionaries did. The thought I had that he wasn't living on at all came to me as a surprise. He was in the ground in Oola with his ancestors. All I had left of him were the memories – like the sounds of his hobnail boots on the cement floor and of his waistcoat, shiny with dribbles.

I had got into the habit of going across the plaza to chew the fat with Doc Novales, one of two local GPs I had come to know very well. He usually had a line of patients waiting for his services, but he always made time for me. I wanted to discuss how I'd outflank any future dehydration, as well as other matters we had become accustomed to talk about. This time he was quite un-Filipino in his directness.

'You Irish run around like bulls, as if you were in a temperate climate. You think by drinking beer you can restore the fluids lost in perspiration. Drink water. I know it's filthy but if you boil it, it's OK.'

'Excuse me, Doc,' I said. 'I never drink beer to restore anything. I just drink it. And gin and tonic, and Scotch, and Tanduay rum. They deaden the pain as well as slake the thirst.'

I was having him on a bit – but only a bit. I wanted him to get used to Irish banter – making light of the serious and being serious about the light. It was something he and most Filipinos I met had difficulty with. They could never work out whether we were serious or not.

'What pain?' Doc asked. 'You now have a pain you have not told me about?'

'Not that kind of pain, Doc. More like confusion . . . Drink makes light of the confusion.'

'Confusion? You have a good job. The people like you. We pay you because we like you.'

'Jesus, Doc . . . Do you ever feel inadequate? Do you ever feel frustrated in medicine? Are there people out there you could cure if you had time and money? What priorities do you have? An aspirin or a drip to save a child's life? Taking a bullet out of one of the mayor's goons who shot himself while pissed? Where do you begin? How do you rationalise it?'

'Why should I rationalise? I have a sign outside this clinic saying DR ERIC NOVALES, MD. If they come to me, I treat them. It is as simple as that. You should put a sign on your *convento*: FR JAMES KENNEDY. The people who come to you will pay you. Not much, but you won't go hungry. You deal with them one by one. If you are good you will get many customers. You are *mabait* (kind). I saw tears in your eyes when the child of Dading was drowned in the fishpond. You do not shout at us like some priests. There are people I cannot cure whom you can cure. Sometimes – do you know this – I inject only water and they feel good. I do not tell you how to do your job but surely it is to make them feel good.'

'Who do I choose to give this feeling of being good to? Only those who come to me? Don't tell me that. I know you're not paid for half your treatments.'

'But I'm happy with what I do. I have no stress. I'm not like you – trying to achieve the impossible in a job. You are always thinking and searching and asking this and that. There are two people in you – the one that smiles and does the work and the one that grits teeth and examines each particle of energy to see if it's properly applied. Learn from us how not to waste body fluids. Even learn from the pace of the carabao. Don't

50

rush past us and excuse yourself because you are chasing some terrific new idea.'

'Am I not treating this moment with you as if it were important?'

'You are, but you are pushing me into your debate about your confusion. I have no solution for you because I do not think like you. I'm only your physician and I will listen to you and once I'm sure you are mentally and physically sound, my job is done. If you want to wrestle with things philosophical, perhaps you should go up on a mountain and not come down until you have thought it all out. Although most of my blood is Spanish, I am Asian. I have to be. I cannot do a day's work here and be in doubt about its validity.'

As I made my way back to the *convento*, the Aglipayan priest, Father de la Rosa, was looking out from the big door of his dilapidated church, which fronted the side of the plaza opposite my aircraft hangar. His congregation was going down and down. His Philippine Independent Church, founded by Gregorio Aglipay in a wave of anti-Spanish nationalism, peeled off from Rome in 1902. Its adherents were only four per cent of the population now.

Pedro and I were competitors for souls.

He gave me a sad sort of wave. No business today either, I figured. The sign recommended by Dr Novales would have suited him. He badly needed the pesos from a few funerals. He had two children and a wife to feed, but was a victim of a cultural oddity of Philippines. As a society, Philippines was deemed to be matriarchal. The old ladies on his church board called the shots for him in church matters; his wife called them for him at home.

He had far less say in his destiny than I.

As well as having Doc as a friend, I also had Juanito Posadas, a most affable man; Leonardo (Narding) Affable, the municipal judge in the next town of Castillejos, who was most unlike a judge because he laughed a lot; and Romy Maningding, whom I called on a lot because my electrics and sound systems were always breaking down. And then there was Doctor Nepomuceno, another GP, droll and direct, and, of course, Conrado. I was very happy to have them around me because there was very little they didn't know about Subic and its people. I suppose too that they had become reliables not only because they spoke and understand English well but because they had experience of the nuances from contact with English-speaking people in their education and professions. One or other of them interpreted attitudes and behaviour for me when, because of my cultural inexperience, I got frustrated at not being able to feel my way through the nods, winks and vibes underlying the apparent passivity of Filipino behaviour. Even my instinct – which works well with the Celts, Yanks and Anglo-Saxons – was utterly unreliable there. After the All Souls incident, I got into an even bigger cultural tangle, only this time I couldn't back down. There was a principle at stake which wasn't merely Asian or European. It was, in my book, a universal principle.

I came home late one night from Manila to find the church lit up and crowded. Every light in the ceiling was on. Food and drink were available outside. The clickety-clack of mah-jong pieces at tables down the side aisles punctuated a steady hum of conversation. It was a wake. In my absence, Mrs Juico had died. She was the mother of the Mayor of Olongapo, who was the second most powerful person, politically, in the province.

The first thing I wondered was who was going to pay the electricity bill. And then I asked, in very un-Filipino language, 'What the hell is going on?'

It was explained to me that Mrs Juico was a very important person and all the stops would have to be pulled out for her burial. Since I wasn't there, Conrado and the 'reliables' had made the decisions and would I go along with them?

'Using the church as an amusement arcade isn't exactly my way of doing things,' I replied, 'but I'll go along with you, except for one item in your programme.

'I can't walk ahead of the cortège to the cemetery. You know why.'

The parish had a system going back to Spanish times in which funeral rites could be administered in various grades of ritual splendour, depending on how much money changed hands. A High Mass, incense, accompaniment of the cortège to the cemetery by priest and acolytes and a sung blessing in the cemetery was top-of-the-range. A few prayers and a sprinkle of holy water, at two pesos, was for the poor – many of whom couldn't even afford a child's coffin, just a simple wooden box tied between two bamboo poles.

It was not in me to continue with this system, for obvious reasons. I arranged that I'd say a funeral Mass for the dead of rich and poor and if the bereaved family wanted to donate money for the church, it would be voluntary and unspecified. But (and here was the catch about the late Mrs Juico) I also arranged that because of the high number of funerals – sometimes three a day – I couldn't do the burial rites at the cemetery.

Conrado had warned me, 'It's going to ruin the parish finances.'

53

'We are all children of God, Conrado, like you reminded me. Are we not all equal in His eyes?' I asked. I could be a smart-ass too.

Doc (who was also playing mah-jong that night) took me aside and explained the facts of Filipino life to me.

'In the Philippines we stay with the dead,' he said.

'So do the Irish,' I answered, 'but we've stopped turning wakes into carnivals.'

'That was no carnival,' Doc said seriously. 'You must understand that our attitude to death is different to yours. You notice how we always have our picture taken with our dead. It is not our custom to be sombre and sad when someone of full years is called away. It is expected of us that we see this woman's spirit off in an ambience of happiness and normality. A little mah-jong helped us to put down the long night, and the coffee and cakes kept us awake. This is no disrespect to you or the Church. The Spanish friars learned this from us. They saw how the Chinese, especially, paid respect to departed ancestors by eating and playing mah-jong beside their tombs. The Spaniards knew that Filipinos will use any excuse for a celebration so they adapted to our ways. You have to adapt too.'

That was a polite kick in the butt for me, a fan of Spanish evangelisation, but one who, when the crunch came, didn't recognise it.

'You may not know,' Doc added, 'that the Chinese and Spanish figure prominently among the ancestors of Mrs Juico. She was also a keen mah-jong player. Up to this you've only seen poor and middle-class funerals. Today you will see how the *ilustrados* do it. And there is something else . . . ' Here Doc was obviously uncomfortable. 'It's about the rule you have made, which is a good rule – not walking to the cemetery, I mean.'

'What about it?' I asked.

'You won't have to do it,' he said softly. 'Ging (Doc's wife) and Ludy (her friend, whose brother was Bishop Gaviola) are gone to Iba for Bishop Byrne. When he comes, everyone will save face.'

Next day, as Doc said, the bishop arrived in his VW with his driver, Delfin, and Paddy Quigley, then chaplain to the mining village of Acoje. The bishop asked me for permission to officiate at the Mass and to walk in the funeral procession to the cemetery. He and Paddy gave Mrs Juico the big treatment. I helped out like an acolyte in the church but didn't walk to the cemetery.

It struck me afterwards that it was most unlikely that anybody noticed. Principles, when confronted with custom and power in the Philippines, last as long as the early-morning fog. And my bishop, who was from Edenderry, County Offaly, serenely went along with them. He, coincidentally, became a Filipino citizen the following year.

4

Dear Annette,

Are you some kind of theologian or what?

I have seriously thought of separating the wheat from the chaff in the job here. I have a workable definition of Christianity. I have an idea of what a priest is and what I should be doing as one. However, I can't put it all together – yet.

I am alone, and any serious separation of wheat from chaff can only remain a plan. I don't choose the agenda for the day; it writes itself. Blessings of jeepneys, tricycles, houses and God knows what else. Why the Filipino needs to have so many things blessed beats me.

Funerals come in unannounced, particularly those of children and babies, especially during the rainy season. Baptisms come in unheralded. Some *ninong* or *ninang* (a godparent, male or female) is available only at a certain time and I won't be the one to screw up a family celebration planned without reference to me. I am forewarned about activities and programmes in the school which need my presence, but give priority to the Catholics in their bare feet.

The catechetical programme in the four municipal public elementary schools needs support and sometimes my presence. There are a couple of weddings every week, although the mayor is doing more of them in his office than a loyal churchman should appreciate. It makes no difference to me. I visit the sick who need me and who have been referred to me by the Legionaries of Mary. I walk around the municipality to explore areas I haven't come across and to practise my Tagalog with the people.

There are municipal programmes to which I am invited at night, as well as CFM (Catholic Family Movement), CWL (Catholic Women's League) and Legion of Mary meetings which I'm supposed to participate in and inspire. I have barrio Masses and I'm involved with the farmers of Manggahan in repairing an irrigation system which the floods and logging upstream have made derelict.

There's a wave of anti-Marcos stuff going on here – most of it underground – since martial law was declared. I discovered that five of the St James teachers were recruited by some ancillary group of the NPA (New People's Army) and are having what were described to me as 'Marxist cell meetings' in the school. I'm in sympathy with their aspirations but I'm unequivocally against secret societies and conspiracies. And I made that quite clear to them.

I keep saying to myself: 'Go along with the flow, James. Go with the fall of ground. You're learning. Sooner or later, you'll make sense out of it.'

With that as a background, let me now answer your two questions, which, in the circumstances, make more sense than you think.

I find it necessary to have a working definition of Christianity before me at all times, otherwise I'd take my eye off the ball and end up all over the place. I sum it up in terms of three scenarios from the New Testament – a desert and two hills.

The temptation in the desert for Christ was his vocation test, when he refused to be bought off or to compromise with evil in the guise of the cute hoor, the manipulator, the exploiter, the con man, the dictator. He had discovered values, radical values, and in this scene he willed to stick by them.

The Beatitudes elaborated on those radical values and were the first public expression of those values to a crowd on a hillside.

The hill of Calvary was the proof of his commitment to his radical values and to his disciples and others who would remain radical.

That's how simple Christianity is, Annette! The word 'radical' keeps cropping up, doesn't it, and it is the last word I'd associate with myself this minute in Subic.

Your second question – what is a priest? – would, I've decided, take me too long to unravel, but I promise you I'll have a go at it when I think more about it against the background of Subic. Being ordained is only symbolic of priesthood, in my view. It's what you do and how you do it that creates priesthood in you. I dislike the word 'priest'. I can't help associating it with cults, secret rituals, witch-doctoring, exclusivity and weird old men dressed up, and I wish there was another word as a job description for what I aspire to be. But it has to be something like the way Christ practised it: sitting on a rock or a grassy knoll explaining eternal truths to people willing to listen, and following this up with a kind of aftercare which is dedicated, patient and kind.

The priesthood has been made so complicated down through the centuries by a succession of popes and their canon lawyers and theologians that the job description now runs off the page. Then add on what my bishop, Harry Byrne, wants of me as a priest, what John Curry, my Columban superior, wants and how 18,000 people in the parish see me – is it any wonder that Doc recommends me to go to the mountain and work it out?

I want to thank you, not only for participating in funding the scholarships, but for becoming involved in the spirit as well as the deed. While I'm not even remotely expressing the reality of this mission thing as I find it, I hope some day to be relaxed and detached enough to talk about it to you. Even then it will be well-nigh impossible.

I often wish we could develop some way of registering the streams of consciousness which lie buried in us so that we could transfer what we really feel and think and notice and resolve. One feels like Zachary in the temple, struck dumb, and only able to say, 'John is his name.'

I have a feeling now that I would enjoy talking to you because you seem to have taken so many bulls by the horns and emerged poised and still fighting. We can become more parochial and complacent out here much more quickly than you – out of sheer tiredness (temperature at 98 degrees for the last two weeks) – and what I miss most of all is hearing that different voice and feeling the sharp edge of a keen discussion.

Finally, I have on record from you: 1 April – £4; 4 April – £5. On behalf of Rosella and Rolando, our scholars, I thank you very sincerely, because I know that in spite of what you say about being lucky, etc., you still need that £9 as much as any middle-class citizen of Merrie England. My best wishes to Purita, Miguel and Inigo and blessings on yourself.

Subic, 23 April 1974

Dear Annette,

I'm going to keep a tight rein on myself for this one. Once again I've had to think long and hard about the questions you put to me in yours of 2 March.

When you say to me, 'You don't think like a priest', is that good or bad? What does a priest think like? Who are you comparing me to? I don't parrot out moral aphorisms or assembly-line spirituality.

A priest I worked with in Dalgan came out here to give the annual retreat. He covered acres of ground, from the Fall to the Redemption, and then on to Vatican II. He quoted more scripture, fathers of the Church, theologians, Vatican documents and lives of the saints than I ever believed could be lumped together in three days. He was an encyclopaedia of spiritual knowledge. What he didn't do was offer a single observation that was his own. I slept during the whole of it.

Oddly enough, he's very subjective and witty on any topic but religion. His problem is like mine used to be – being so overawed by the message of salvation that I thought it should work independently of any input from me. I was only the gramophone; the message was the record on the turntable.

Now I know that doesn't work.

That may seem obvious to you, but to those of us

who were drilled in orthodoxy, in the danger of heresies and false philosophies, good preaching wasn't that simple. There was always the fear that if you trusted your own judgement or your own interpretation, you would deviate from the truth.

It was through the study of art in Chicago (I slipped it in under the heading of 'Design and Print' and no one was any the wiser) that I saw the light. The element which, more than anything else, makes a painter is the ability to study techniques of the great painters over every period and to be influenced by them. Then, at a certain point, it is necessary to forget all about them and to paint from what is inside the budding painter's self. That made sense to me.

I have studied the 'great masters' of Catholic thought as well as Lutherans (Dietrich Bonhoeffer is my Van Gogh), Baptists, Anglicans, Methodists and so on. They have pointed me in this direction, and until that, I wondered if I had a mind of my own at all. It was when I began to trust the *Homo sapiens* within myself that I saw I had a part to play in the record as well as being the gramophone.

Is this the way the Holy Spirit works?

That's where I'm at now. I'm also aware that I have to read the Scriptures and must listen to the bishop (only if he makes sense, of course!) to keep myself from becoming the Pope of Subic, to keep the balance between the subjective and the objective. In my communication with you, I have been exceedingly subjective. You're ten thousand miles away and I have to talk this way to someone – so much is prompting me out here. And I do value your feedback. That, probably, is what gave rise to your next question – 'Many of your friends seem to be nuns; have you a teeny-weeny bit of a fetish about them?'

That observation hit a sore spot because I have been sniggered at about being a 'nun's man' by some of the hard men – the card-playing, whiskey-drinking types of Columban. I know your remark is tongue-in-cheek and you don't mean it like them. Here are a few observations.

I've never heard anyone admit it, but there are odd attitudes among priests towards nuns. Some I know are misogynists and conceal a version of it for the woman as nun. These men are also authoritarian. They are chauvinists for Jesus and have no idea they are. They use the obedience principle and the command structure of the Church in order to be effective in their jobs. When they say Mass in the convent, they scarcely greet – not to mention thank – the sister sacristan or the novice who brings them their solitary breakfast in the parlour. To them the Church is a pyramid of subservient echelons and the nuns are somewhere down there. But as for sharing ideas with a nun about a parish issue such as finance – 'Sure what would they know about that?'

All nuns and priests are indoctrinated in the necessity of obedience to superiors. Nothing new in that. Any soldier knows that good leadership can create a cohesive force, which helps the group to survive.

Obedience, in spite of this rubbish thing about it being one of the big three virtues of religious life, is just a controlling mechanism. It has the same purpose in the Church as in the army, only it is more subtly administered. The trick is to see the person of Christ in one's superior, and by obeying Christ in him or her, you obey the superior.

Isn't that some sleight of mind?

I've always seen a need to respond to honest and competent leadership without any of this crap.

I have also served diligently under a superior or two in whom I couldn't see Jesus – in a fit.

It is necessary for me to say what I've said because the Church is as much responsible for clerical chauvinism as the individuals who practise it. Most priests, however, take a neutral course. They see nuns as women whom they have been trained to be wary of, and nowadays, with habits thrown off and nice legs exposed, they may have good reason to be wary. Ask any nun for an honest answer to that!

Many of them do not consider nuns to be quite normal women in the same way that many priests do not consider each other to be quite normal men when they take off the blinkers to look at the whole celibacy thing.

This doesn't mean that they're homosexual or frigid. It's just that the following thought may cross their minds: Why should this handsome, talented person leave home and the money with which to be trained in another profession, reject heterosexual love and choose to gain fulfilment through what ordinary people would call deprivation? To give a positive answer to the question takes a huge leap of faith and I often wonder how much faith is really around.

Ask me about that some time.

The minority of priests treat nuns as equal co-workers in a similar type of job. The older ones here in Zambales, like Mick Donoher and Paddy Quigley and Tom Connolly in Manila, are respectful and civilised about it; the younger ones have a healthy brother-and-sister attitude to it. These are only off-the-cuff observations and therefore generalities.

I'm clear enough on my own attitude though.

Like most attitudes, this one began at home. My mother never had much difficulty in steering me around rural chauvinism towards an attitude of respect for and courtesy to women as equals, but different. I must admit that we never got this hogwash about 'woman as temptress' in Dalgan Park. If anything, the whole thing was played down. I do remember a warning given by one of our two spiritual directors, Father Harris, an ascetic-looking Kerryman.

'It is not the flashy woman you should be wary of, boy, but the mousy one who may be the president of your Legion of Mary.'

None of us, of course, believed him. Being seduced, for us, then in our early twenties, was something that was going to be tried on only by a stripper or some lady of the night – and in Hong Kong. It couldn't possibly happen in the company of virtuous women with whom we had so much in common.

I took all the cautions about celibacy quite seriously, and it wasn't until I was twenty-six that I bit the dust for the first time.

She was a Dublin girl who was part of an exuberant gang of ours in Chicago and we used to swim on Sunday afternoons in Lake Michigan. She could have had me for breakfast, but her integrity as a Catholic and her respect for the priesthood made her play it down and eventually put the lid on it. We never did more than hold hands.

When I returned to Ireland in 1962, I told J.W. about

64

it, coming back from Baltray, after our first game of golf together in two years. Rather than give me absolution, because I was truly repentant, he pointed to the Franciscan Friary and said, 'Get thee in there and be properly shriven.'

It would seem that he wanted me to suffer a bit.

I was very nervous. My palms were sweaty when I knelt at the prie-dieu in the bare parlour. I had rehearsed my story to make it as innocuous as possible but, of course, I couldn't avoid the substantial and, in hindsight, extravagant statement, 'I fell in love with a woman.'

A gaunt old priest with another Kerry accent came out and put on the stole. When I had my stuttering, sad story finished there was a silence of about fifteen seconds. Then I heard him clicking his tongue.

'Tsuck, tsuck, tsuck. What will I do with you at all?'

Where I got the presence of mind from, I don't know, but I did answer, 'Nothing at all, Father. Have a nice day.'

And then I walked out, closing the door gently behind me.

I think I forgot to ask J.W. for his absolution. I felt I had repented enough.

The Chicago experience had taught me a lesson. How unfair it was of a priest to develop a love relationship with a woman whom he cannot marry but who, herself, has no restrictions against marriage. I tended after that to steer clear of the girls, and did so for five years, until Alice hugged me in the sacristy.

Well, it took place on holy ground, after all, and Alice was not really a girl!

In the mid-sixties, the common cause of *aggiornamento* in the Church brought a lot of nuns and priests together at meetings and seminars. They began to appreciate one another's roles more, sharing the same aims and the same restrictions. Many personalities shrouded by repression opened up, as personality and individualism was encouraged. It was in that milieu I met Alice, and you could say she was repressed, having gone into a convent as a boarder at fourteen, never to leave it. I will keep you up to date with the story as it develops. By the way, why haven't you ticked me off about it? Do you approve?

So now, have I a fetish about nuns or not?

Since then I've become close friends with many other nuns – Kitty O'Flaherty, Anna Brady, Thu Thieu, Josepha Aldana, I think of immediately – who are intelligent and dedicated people, far more intelligent and dedicated than the run-of-the-mill priests I've worked with. I see them as co-workers offering the feminine viewpoint in a man's world. I don't see their veils or their vows. I see people who want to be in the front lines of Christendom approaching the twenty-first century. If I go soft on one of them and she on me, she's taking the same risks with her vows as I am. Neither of us can be accused of exploiting the other.

I have good friends among the men too, by the way.

On the nuns-and-women thing, there's another dimension presenting itself here in Philippines which is adding a bit of piquancy to life – an indefinable sexuality in the women, which doesn't confront one on a frosty morning in Surbiton. I don't mean they are promiscuous. They have far fewer hang-ups about their sexuality than Irish women do. Recently I was preparing to take a group of catechists to the beach and one shouted in to me from the road that she couldn't travel.

'Why not?' I asked.

'Because I'm having my period,' she shouted back.

The chaperone system is alive and well also. There is a warmth and cuddliness and innocence and vivacity in them which invites investigation. Apropos of that, I've been planting rice recently with one of the second-year classes – a special project of our school.

Our boss is a sixteen-year-old girl called Connie Jose. She fascinates me. She is the 'Virgin' of the great painters. She is Mother Earth springing up from the ooze of the paddy-field rice in human form, and a very gracious human form at that. She was field mother to us all – even to the older and bigger boys (all reluctant volunteers) of her class – because she has the authority and knowledge that great mothers possess. It is a most impressive gift.

Apart from developing a pain in the back from all the bending and squishing around, I enjoyed it immensely. What was wonderful was the feeling of walking barefoot in eight-inch-deep, warm, oozy mud. Try it some time, instead of putting it on your face, as women, I'm told, do nowadays. It's almost a sexual experience.

Finally, how can I write letters to you if I only reply to your first sentence and don't even tell you about my glorious mission in Subic. So, a warning: don't bring up the subject of nuns or women or mud until I get a bit of work done. Then I'll tell you about the two nuns who practically fought it out on a beach south of here about which was to get swimming lessons first from the parish priest. In my opinion, he wasn't worth fighting over.

I found out later that both knew how to swim.

I'm now going to bed.

5

You cannot lose your way in Zambales because there is only one road running from north to south. It is a ninety-mile long, skinny province, predominantly coastline, with Santa Cruz, a farming and mining municipality, at the extreme north, and Olongapo City – called 'Sin City' when it was host to the biggest US Navy base in the Far East – at the extreme south. To the west is the South China Sea and to the east, the high Zambales Mountains. There is no road going over the mountains from west to east, to the adjoining provinces of Tarlac and Pampanga. Zambales is punctuated in the middle by the capital town, Iba. North of Iba are the towns of Palauig, Masinloc, Candelaria and Santa Cruz. South from Iba are the towns of Botolan, Cabangan, San Felipe, San Narciso, San Antonio, Castillejos, Subic and Olongapo City.

In secular terms, these are municipalities, but, of course, in religious parlance, they are parishes – all manned by Columbans, who in the seventies were Irish, American, Australian and New Zealander, with a sprinkling of young Filipino priests being trained to take over. Today, some thirty years later, the Columbans are administering only one parish and all the others are being staffed by Filipino priests under their own Filipino bishop.

In my mind I go back through the list of Columbans running the parishes and the schools then. Most had twenty years' experience. They were set in their practices, knew the ropes, and their parishes were active and well run, much like parishes in Ireland, England or the US. I was their generation – the pre-Vatican II generation – yet I was not one of them. I was a newcomer, and I shared my lack of experience with another newcomer to the province, Seamus Connolly, whom the Filipinos call 'Saymus'. They have difficulty with the 'sh's, just as we have difficulty with their 'ng's.

Without his company, the year at language school in Manila would have been excruciating. He was the new breed, ten years younger than me and better educated in philosophy and theology. He was apprenticed to an affable, laid-back Clareman in Masinloc called Donal O'Dea, and was finding the going tough.

Seamus couldn't leave things alone. He had to make judgements about them. I think it was only then things begin to exist in relation to him. He judged everything – mosquitoes, street signs, theology, my performance, the Columban Fathers, nuns, the world economy. He analysed them, ran them through whatever open mind was within earshot, redefined them and packaged them for future use. His problem (apart from the bad water in Masinloc and periodic bouts of the runs) was that, according to him, there weren't enough open, energetic minds around, only a lot of tired, complacent missionaries.

In another person, this flair could have been threatening. In Seamus, it made life within his radius at language school exciting, provocative and utterly wearing for anyone trying to understand and keep register of his thoughts. It was as if this frenzy of thinking happened because he was afraid his mind would close down prematurely and he wouldn't be able to unravel enough of the mysteries that surrounded us, and the problems that beset us.

I openly admit his questions made me think. His boundless curiosity and provocation were very stimulating for me but raised the hackles of some of our more self-assured and opinionated older missionaries. Then he had more questions than answers and I hadn't the slightest doubt that when the answers began to come he would act. That's what made him so different from the armchair professors I'd been listening to all my life.

What made him and many of his contemporaries different is that they were educated outside the Columban cocoon at secular universities and I hoped then that our superiors would realise that it was this education which would let all the genies out of their bottles eventually. Whether they would encourage it and build around it or whether they would fight it to retain the status quo would determine the future of the Missionary Society of St Columban.

Seamus was far from happy one day I drove north and dropped in to Masinloc. O'Dea happened to be away and Seamus was nowhere to be seen. I was having a cold San Miguel and was looking out to sea from the *sala* window when I heard the slow, rhythmic drumming and the funereal notes of a brass band. Then a funeral procession came into view, heading for the church. The coffin was on an open four-wheeled carriage, which was being pulled by the mourners. Instead of shafts, the carriage had two long ropes with a dozen or so men to each rope, each team of men about three yards apart.

In the middle, in the boiling sun, was Seamus. He had a heavy cope on, was red-faced and sweating profusely. I didn't go down but let him finish. When he came upstairs to join me in the *sala*, I started to laugh, because somehow, the image of Seamus performing a very pedestrian function, participating solemnly and *en robe* in a mediaeval Spanish funeral ritual in the midday sun in Philippines, and to the music of a brass band, seemed so out of keeping with his liberation-theology ideas that it looked like theatre.

'That one cost them a hundred pesos,' he said cynically. 'It's the deluxe version. The problem here is that very few people can afford a hundred pesos and we are supporting a class system, even among the dead.'

Seamus in his cope in Masinloc was caught like a fly in a web of culture where neither the Aristotelian thinker nor the liberation theologian could contend with the 'losing face' factor in Asia. His perfectly logical comment about class among the dead was quite acceptable for Frass in Glenamaddy, County Galway, where he came from, but made no sense at all in Masinloc, Zambales, where image – face – was everything.

We only suspected that then. We were too ignorant about the cultures of Asia (Philippines, deep down, being a microcosm of it) and, perhaps, too arrogant about our own superiority to be convinced of it. Of all the places I've ever been to or read about, Philippines stands out in one respect: it has an immense capacity to tolerate and absorb fools. Filipinos never fight with you or scold you for being wrong. It would be too embarrassing for you and that's about the worst thing that could happen to you in their value system. I know a few Columbans who escalated to fame in Philippines because of this, but back in Ireland, with responsibility, their talents were found to have been inflated.

There was one night near the end of my term in Subic when a carload of young but fairly seasoned Columbans dropped into Subic on their way to Pangasinan and Baguio. Among them were some Americans and Australians. After dinner, the gin and San Miguel flowed freely.

Normally, on occasions such as parish fiestas when Columbans got together, the pack of cards was brought out, because it was not customary to talk shop. As a matter of fact, any discussion of a serious nature about the apostolate was avoided like the plague. This time, the talk got freer and freer, and because all were the younger generation, it kept going, and it was very much about how each of us felt we were doing in our parishes. There was a devil-may-care attitude about the drinking, and the talking got close to the bone.

Seamus, who happened to be visiting, made sure of that, of course. Some time in the early morning, one of us who shall be nameless freaked out. There is no other word for it, except that it was a coherent, impassioned freaking out. A dam broke somewhere, releasing suppressed torrents of anger and confusion about Philippines and its culture which took us behind the veil of Filipino agreeableness and hospitality and let us see what it was doing to this guy, who was holding on desperately to the values, not only of his own culture, but of the Western Jesus culture.

He was sitting on the floor in a corner and there was a row of empty San Miguel beer bottles in front of him. The scene was like one from Joseph Wambaugh's *The Choirboys*, in which a group of New York cops, stressed from the job, meet periodically and let it all hang out.

'I think you are all daft. The question is not about liberation theology, or Third World development – or even about Jesus and His Kingdom. The thing is, I'm going nowhere. The difference between you guys and me is that I know I'm going nowhere.

'"What did you think of my sermon today, Juanita?"

'"Very nice, Fader!"

'"What do you think we should do about that guy in the Holy Name Society, Juanito?"

'"It's up to you, Fader."

'You know and I know, that for Filipinos, to disagree is a breach of etiquette. So, if you have no disagreement, you can have no argument and no consensus. Without a dialectic of possible disagreement, you can't even begin to discuss liberation theology or development or Jesus in the tabernacle. You'd be better off to stay in bed all day, and preferably with some cuddly *dalaga* (unmarried girl), so as not to waste your time completely.'

'Hear, hear!' we all shouted enthusiastically.

'Have any of you ever heard a sin from a Filipino in the confessional? I haven't. No Filipino ever said, "I did this." He beats around the bush and puts up one smokescreen after another like *pakikisama* and *bahala na*. Admission of guilt is watered down because of this fucking *pakikisama* – because the individual is watered down to some common denominator acceptable to family and peer group. It is watered down to such an extent that the individual doesn't exist any more.

'And if it isn't *pakikisama*, it's the fatalism of *bahala na* that takes them off the hook. "It just happened that I stuck a knife in this guy's back. It kind of went in by itself." Am I right? "The lamp fell." He wouldn't dream of saying, "I dropped it." "The tape recorder got lost." It was stolen, of course, and rather than point the finger at someone, the tape recorder just walked away by itself and decided to get lost.

'So, brothers, old-time Spanish Catholicism with its colour and ritual and saints is still the name of the game. You guys talk from your altars about justice and the poor, and expect it to change minds and then society? It will take ten times longer

73

than you think and you don't have the time anyway. The Filipino priests will have taken over by then and they will do it their way.

'What's that guy's name . . . Horatio de la Costa SJ writes about Filipino values. He has a list of them, but the daddy of them all is *hiya*. It anaesthetises everyone in sight, preventing people from calling a spade a spade. So, are we here to call a spade a spade or are we not? The SJ, cute man, solves the problem by calling the religion of the Filipino 'split-level Christianity'. One part to suit the east, one part for the west. One kind for you, one kind for us. Mammy's handy little recipe. Bollocks! It would take a Jesuit to think that one up, wouldn't it?

'You know what I think? I think Filipinos should belong to a non-conflict religion like Buddhism, or Taoism, and we should all go home.'

'Hear, hear!' we all cheered.

'I'm not finished yet,' he said.

'I want to get back to the complications these dusky, feminine, cuddly, scantily clad, adorable *dalagas* bring into our sterile and useless lives . . . '

'Your time is up,' I said. 'Let's hear from someone else.'

They departed an hour or so after curfew lifted and headed north without sleep, on a breakfast of coffee and *pan de sal*. They thought they might have lunch and siesta in Lingayen – that is, if they didn't call to see the guys in Iba . . . or Duffin in Santa Cruz . . . or go up to the mines in Acoje to see John Moran.

Connie Jose is over forty years old by now. Perhaps she is missing a few of her lovely teeth, because the toothpaste smile was never a priority amid the realities of Manggahan. By now she will have five or six children and her perfect olive skin will have become darkened and wrinkled by the sun and by the cares of survival.

Perhaps she is no longer in Subic. Her father's land would have been covered thickly in volcanic ash after the eruption of Mount Pinatubo in 1991. I can't remember when I picked her out in my mind from six hundred other girls in St James High School and then, ever after that, looked for her in the schoolyard at playtime from my veranda – just to reassure myself that she was there.

Once she was there, never quite at ease in her black shoes and white ankle socks, I felt all was well with the world. It was a strange sort of secret attachment, as if she became, for me, the beautiful earth woman, symbolising all the women of the archipelago. I felt she could make the earth grow what she wanted it to grow, that she retained the gift of being able to save the world from hunger.

I knew another Filipina like that, a dark, nimble girl from Ilocos, who came to our house in Dublin many years after. We were on a tributary of the Boyne during summer, and next thing, she was in the water, clothes and all, excited at the amount of freshwater shrimp she saw and caught with her hands. I was a fly fisherman for years in the Boyne area and never knew they existed.

Connie was sixteen and in second-year D, which meant that in the streaming system there were three other classes allegedly brighter. She had become a vital link for me with Subic, like another student, Rosella de la Paz. With Rosella the breakthrough came when we discussed drama and crafts.

Connie was different. She was shy, deferential, not great at

English but, on her subject, her face and body came alive with interest and confidence.

Her subject was farming.

Being proud of and articulate about her father's occupation made her an exception in Subic, where farming was regarded as lowly, and many of the children I talked to would be uncomfortable in admitting it as the livelihood of their parents. Perhaps that is not true of the Ilocanos and the Ifugao who seemed to specialise proudly in it but it was true of many people in southern Zambales, who were more impressed by the blue-collar attitudes that came across from American educational textbooks.

Connie's father was a farmer in Manggahan – a very good one, according to Juanito Posadas, the Municipal Agricultural Adviser. Mr Jose had even rented mountain land in Naugsol, three kilometres behind Manggahan, where the Zambales Mountains started to rise, and planted upland rice on it, to supplement his crop of paddy-field rice near his house.

Connie delighted in walking the three kilometres of paths to their fields in Naugsol in her bare feet, to help her father. Posadas, who would have recommended diversification into upland rice, was probably behind it. He was a top-class man, as I found out later. Now that I think of it, too, it must have been Elisabeth Molina, her teacher, who brought Connie to my notice. I was probably whinging about honky-tonk Subic and my inability to establish a common ground with shopkeepers, whorehouse owners and American wannabes. Elisabeth was astute and a girl you could talk to.

To this day, Connie has no way of knowing how important she was to me. She gave me a way out, a direction away from ritual Catholicism per se and, at a crucial time, the chance to integrate myself for the first time into the real life of the Philippines.

Farming was real life. I had a common denominator with it from Brackile. From there I could begin my work – whatever it turned out to be – as well as picking up pieces. All the time, the problem had been that I didn't know where or how to begin. The farmers of Manggahan didn't go to Mass but they were the same as myself – once we got rid of the cultural and religious excess baggage.

Like the friars, I was there for the rest of my life. I wasn't a journeyman. I wanted to grow roots and live with a tribe. I was very uncomfortable with the impersonal sort of priesthood – the journeyman priest, here today and gone tomorrow. No loyalties except to his bishop and his superior.

Christ did have his own tribe. He was one of the people He walked among. And His pedagogy and behaviour were far from being impersonal. I would start communicating with the farmers on common agricultural values and with respect and assurance. Then, being on safe philosophical as well as theological ground, I could go on from there.

In the end it never turned out like that. It was only a fairy story. As with the college magazine in Dalgan, all it did was keep my mind and dreams alive for a while.

The parish owned two hectares of land bordering the main road in the barrio of Manggahan. It was leased to two tenants for six bags of rice each per year. One was a good tenant. He got maximum yield out of it and delivered his six bags without argument. The other was a disaster. He was fond of the bottle. His crop, when he thought of sowing it, was unfertilised and ended up an eyesore to passers-by. We never got any rice from him. I had given him money for fertiliser and he drank it.

77

Posadas recommended me to take the land back and use it as an agricultural project for the school. 2D weren't that interested in the books anyway. 'Let's see what they can do,' Posadas suggested.

The laws between tenant farmers and landowners in Philippines are strict, so it took us (mainly Juanito) months of negotiation to reach a settlement. I paid over a sum of money and one hectare reverted back to us, for the use of the school.

Posadas was our adviser, of course, but because it was a school project I made Connie the boss. The boss over myself, who intended to participate because I knew nothing about rice-growing, and the boss over her classmates, boys as well as girls.

She had a natural authority, based on knowledge and love of her subject, which managed the project to a successful conclusion – to the day on the shiny concrete of the school basketball court when she supervised the threshing by hand and the dividing of the grain among her classmates.

She had kept the secret entrusted to her at the beginning by Juanito and myself. The rice seed was 'miracle rice', straight from the Rice Research Institute in Los Banos. It would be its first test run in Zambales. It was harvested after three months, whereas the surrounding crop took four.

The farmers in Manggahan shook their heads in disbelief at her powers. Connie only smiled at them, a lovely Mona Lisa smile which I can still see in my mind's eye.

6

James the Apostle, patron of Spain, must have come to his adopted country's rescue during some confrontation with the Moors of North Africa, because his life-size effigy in my church was both terrifying and awe-inspiring. James was on horseback, in brocaded velvet and cheap jewels. He had an eight-foot lance in his right hand and with it he was administering the *coup de grâce* to a pair of Moors who had become entangled between the horse's forelegs. That made him *Matamoros*, the Moor killer.

This statue of painted wood rested on an eighteen-inch-high wooden dais, which, with the addition of shafts at each end, could be hauled in procession round the town on the shoulders of the menfolk on the feast of James the Apostle, 25 July.

The plinth, with its statue on top, stayed in the church when it was not doing the rounds of the town. To keep it out of harm's way, it was raised six feet off the ground and rested on another plinth, which could have been a wooden side altar, a survivor from the old Spanish church, courtesy of Ned McKenna.

I didn't realise James was such an all-rounder until I came out one morning for the six o'clock Mass half an hour earlier than usual and spotted Mrs Soledad before she saw me. She was sitting on the horse, James's pillion passenger, and she was

79

rubbing either James or the horse – I forget which – and then rubbing her thigh where she had the rheumatism. She was six feet up, and how she got up so high without the aid of a ladder I haven't worked out to this day.

Mrs Soledad got up at four every morning, opened her stall in the market, handed it over to some assistant and was in church praying for an hour before Mass began. She was a quiet, shy woman in her fifties and often surprised me with the bundle of pesos she secretly handed over to me for the church. I ducked back into the *convento* without her seeing me and returned at my normal time. Mrs Soledad was back at her seat, down the church (never up front with the others), praying away as usual. She was the lady who was looking after John O'Brien's grave.

I was at breakfast later, trying to work out where Mrs Soledad's unusual devotion fitted into the documents of Vatican II. I had a well-thumbed and annotated paperback of all the documents, and I read them – unlike most of the guys, who kept them in bookshelves, or used them to keep the table with the short leg steady.

These documents laid the groundwork for new approaches to being a Christian, none more so than paragraph sixteen from the section on the Church, which basically said that people could go to heaven without being Catholic or even Christian. That took the heat off me in the redemption business, but unfortunately didn't take the heat off me in the human-condition business, which was what an element of Subic was beginning to be all about – poverty, exploitation, malnutrition, sometimes hunger.

But I could do something immediately about an architectural problem relating to the parish's patron.

There was a three-feet-wide by ten-feet-long concrete ledge left for a statue of James over the front entrance of the new church, but I first had to ask myself could I support another *matamoros* version of James up there while there was a guerrilla war going on in Mindanao between the government and the Moros – perhaps seen as another Christian–Muslim conflict. It would be provocation rather than reconciliation. I had an axe to grind in my own soul too about *Matamoros*.

Had there been peace there on 19 October 1970 – shortly after I arrived in Philippines – Martin Dempsey, my own age and a Columban from Dublin, might never have been shot dead. A settlement between the Philippine government and the Moros was arrived at only in 1996. There was peace in Mindanao until Abu Sayef (a Muslim militant faction with links to Al Qaeda) began to stir up trouble in the mid-nineties.

I flew the six hundred miles to Martin's funeral on an ex-Aer Lingus Fokker from Manila to Davao and by single-engined Cessna to the grass airstrip on the Lobregat plantation beside Balabagan where the murder took place. I saw the bullet marks in the end wall of the L-shaped, one-storey high school which he administered for 350 students, both Muslim and Catholic.

The gross, animal stupidity of his death had a very demoralising effect on me. His killers, both students of the school, were sons of the Muslim mayor, fourteen and seventeen years old respectively. The fourteen-year-old boy had been verbally corrected by Martin for misbehaviour during the pre-class flag ceremony. In Ireland, he would have been called a 'young pup'. The boy got annoyed (it was reported that he had been to Mecca and had therefore become a *haji*) and reported the affair to his seventeen-year-old brother. Both threatened to kill Martin and left the school. Martin carried on, unperturbed.

A short time later, both returned to the school, armed with revolver and carbine. Martin was getting into his jeep when he saw them coming across the playground towards him. He asked them to come into the office and talk it over. From ten feet away they riddled him with bullets and he died instantly.

Neither was ever brought to justice, nor, to my knowledge, was there ever an attempt to do so. I did hear that payment was offered for Martin's loss to the bishop, who, with thinly disguised contempt, turned it down with words like, 'Mindanao couldn't hold enough money to compensate for Martin.'

My version of the killing and the funeral was published in *The Far East*, which censored any mention of the Muslim dimension. Not even mention of the tangible hostility and fear on the faces of the people peering out from the Muslim houses among the coconut trees as we followed Martin's coffin to the church. The harsh realities in the Church are often sacrificed to politics.

Martin was a good friend, *The Far East*'s most prolific photographer in the Philippines. No assignment was too awkward for him. He was a brave man, too, to live in a divided community and to work for the education of all. In 2001, Rufus Halley, another Columban, was shot dead between Balabagan and Malabang. His contribution to Christian–Muslim dialogue was immense. The same blind, militant ignorance brought about his death, and, as in Dempsey's case, no one was prosecuted and jailed for the crime.

Turning the other cheek to those Muslims who practise a perverted version of Islam – with their jihads and fatwas – does neither of the two great religions any good.

So I made my pitch at all the Sunday Masses and, more out of respect for Martin than for anything else, suggested another version of James (also authentic) for the plinth – James the Pilgrim, or *Santiago Peregrino*. I had read Michener's *Iberia* and discovered that the all-rounder, James, had a major stake in the famous mediaeval pilgrimage to Compostella. Among my audience, however, there was no great enthusiasm for the new concept of James the Pilgrim, with staff and satchel. And they weren't about to put their hands in their pockets either, I supposed.

There is always one faithful soul in a parish who will go through fire and water for her parish priest, and Mrs Lesaca, who saw my point, promised to pay for the new statue.

There is also a man everywhere who can do anything, if you look hard enough – even make a statue.

I had acquired a five-feet-high safe of quarter-inch steel after a clean-out of the US base in San Miguel. The only problem was, it was locked, and I didn't have the combination. There was a man who would open it, I was told. He came one day in his bare feet, asked for a one-eight-inch steel bit, a hand-turned drill, a piece of wire and a torch. He had the safe opened in fifteen minutes and politely turned his back while I reset it with my own combination.

The man who came to make the statue was also in his bare feet and had no tools whatever. He told me he wanted a two-foot-by-two-foot block of wood as a base, an eight-foot-long piece of half-inch iron, to act as a sort of spine, rolls of wire and fine rabbit mesh, a bag of cement and some fine sand. All these were provided and I gave him my drawing to follow. Within a week, James the Pilgrim was alive and eight feet tall in Subic, but was never hoisted onto his plinth in my time, because the front of the church wasn't finished.

I saw a photo of him a few years ago, though. He was on his ten-foot-wide ledge over the front door and he looked all wrong. He was spindly and, architecturally and design-wise, didn't fit the position.

Matamoros would have looked majestic though.

83

There was a small timber veranda off the *sala* at the back of the *convento*. It was over the storeroom where we kept the rice and sacks of US Aid cereals used as emergency rations for the poor. It faced the schoolyard and the main road, one hundred metres down a narrow street of private houses. It was lovely to sit there with a cool gin and lime at evening time as the sun went down, and watch the starlings fly in from the fields to roost among the coconut trees.

It was also a place from which to study the movements of people in the quiet of the evening. Instead of windows, most of the houses in Subic had sliding shutters inlaid with capiz shells, which were closed at bedtime and opened at cockcrow.

We saw into one another's *salas* without any embarrassment and sometimes waved at one another.

The short street had fascinated me since the mayor's truck dumped a load of gravel in the middle of it. Originally a metre high, the pile blocked the street and was obviously meant to be distributed to fill the huge potholes after the typhoon rain. Two weeks passed and it was still there, but now flattened in places, where jeepneys and tricycles drove over it. Why the people of the street suffered the inconvenience and didn't fill the holes themselves amazed me. I had thought of sending out the lads of 2F to do it, but resisted the temptation. I wanted to see what would happen.

Then one evening the impasse seemed about to be broken. A man came out of his house with a wheelbarrow and shovel. The monsoon rain had been pouring down for hours – never a deterrent to outdoor work, because typhoon rain is not cold rain and the only clothes needed to work in it are pants or shorts, a T-shirt and flip-flops.

'So there is one just man on Claro Street,' I said to myself.

He went to the heap, filled up his barrow, and instead of heading towards a pothole, wheeled around into his own garden, from whence he never appeared again.

The most positive of all the values in the Filipino value system is *bayanihan*. *Bayan* is a place or a home or a town, the same as *baile* in Irish. *Bayanihan* is when the people get together to help one another, as in moving house, and planting and harvesting rice. There is no difference between it and the Irish word *meitheal*, which was alive and well when I was growing up. Like the *meitheal* in Ireland, the *bayanihan* is less practised now in Philippines. But the fact that the people of Claro Street didn't organise themselves for the common good didn't mean that *bayanihan* was dead. It only proved that it is not a spontaneous coming together of a community. Like the *meitheal*, it is confined to certain formal community events which have roots in the rural past.

The Filipino value which emerged in Claro Street was *kanya kanya*, which, roughly translated, means 'every man for himself'. Filipinos do not have the British or French or German sense of national pride when it comes to keeping the town or the street spick and span. Society is focussed on the extended family and any responsibility outside of that is somebody else's problem.

It was part of my long-term job in Subic to change that, and I was not looking forward to it. As a matter of fact, I had no idea how to go about it.

I took one last look down Claro Street, because Tony, the cook, had signalled it was suppertime, and I saw the red Renault 4 turning the corner and driving at speed over the flattened heap of gravel. Seamus usually arrived in a cloud of dust, red-faced, with sweat pouring off him. This evening he drove into the yard in typhoon rain and when he came upstairs said, 'I've got myself appointed to work with you. I don't know if that's going to be good for you or good for me.'

The rain was dripping off his dark-blonde hair, which was plastered to his ears and neck in shiny ringlets. He looked down from the *sala* at his battered Renault 4 below.

'That friggin' car,' he said. 'I couldn't close the window. Should have bought a pony and trap instead. What's for supper?'

'Have a drink first,' I said. 'I need to steady my nerves after your news.'

The main reason I was delighted to have Seamus with me (couldn't tell him that, of course) was that he was a thinker. Like all priests I know, he didn't reveal anything about his spiritual life or what passed for a sex life.

Unlike most Columbans, he had wide-ranging and very educated views about the Church and its mission. He wasn't tied down by any missionary precedents, hagiography, the Fathers of the Church or our 'holy founders'. He looked at evangelisation through twenty-first-century eyes – through the eyes of Hans Kung, Karl Rahner, Gustavo Gutierrez – in part because of his years of studying philosophy at UCD.

In another time he would be classified in Ireland as half mad – an affectionate term for one who is gifted intellectually, very direct and a bit non-conformist. The 'mad' half of him comes from Frass in County Galway – the part of him which gets quickly bored by bullshit and waffle, especially if it comes out patronisingly and complacently from some of our twenty-year men. At the fiesta in Santa Cruz, Kieran Heneghan was called out to some road accident and when he got back, Seamus said to him, 'If you ever find me dying on the roadside like that, don't dream of bending over me with your black box of magic tricks.'

He had a habit of playing the *enfant terrible* to force a reaction out of people who didn't want to react. Being patronised as 'the young man' by older guys who 'knew it all' drove him daft.

In Singalong, Manila, during our time at the language school, Gussie Rowe had just come from the airport, having flown in from some parish in Negros for his two-week vacation. Sitting across from him at seven o'clock dinner was Seamus.

Gussie oozed the authority of a master of God's universe and began to share the most recent story of his labours in the Lord's vineyard. He detailed his works in the parish that morning: two funeral Masses, two jeepneys blessed and the Confessions of every child in the schoolyard heard – just in case any of them went plunging into hell while Gussie was away.

The silence that followed was courteous, but the brethren quickly shifted to an issue of real importance – a discussion about the Munster football final the previous Sunday. Gussie was a Kerryman and the change of subject was respectfully close to his heart. Seamus, however, didn't give it time to settle. He plunged in with, 'The sacramental actions of 95 per cent of Columban priests in the Philippines are just voodoo, pure magic.'

Gussie rose up, his face turned purple, and for an instant, he gripped and lifted his chair as if he was about to fling it across the table at Seamus. Seamus had had a few beers, of course, during the holy hour before dinner, but drink never made him discourteous nor any more irreverent than he was when he was on *calamansi* (lime) juice. Seamus, afterwards, was convinced that it was the word 'magic' which lit the fuse in Gussie and which firmly tied him and the brethren to 'the long list of priests, witch doctors, sorcerers, mullahs and rabbis who, ever since the first humanoid, had tried to placate God with water, fire, blood or words.'

What made Seamus and his contemporaries so confident was that they had Vatican II on their side, along with the modern theologians. What made them so confrontational was that they had just left a seminary where they had lost the battle for change with the authorities but had honed their fighting skills. They saw a kind of civil war going on within the Church, the issues of which were crystallising in the mission countries of Africa, Asia and Latin America around new approaches to evangelisation.

Generals were becoming privates and privates were becoming generals – depending where you were – in a struggle over orthodoxy in the wake of Vatican II. Men and women who had spent their lives diligently administering schools and sacraments were being referred to by the new breed as 'voodoo merchants' because so much of religious activity was taken up by ritual, *ex opere operato* spirituality, and sacramentals. They, in turn, used the ecclesiastical structures to keep the upstarts – the first and maybe the only generation of twentieth-century priests and nuns to be properly educated – out of the seats of power and at bay.

It wasn't long before he was pacing the *sala* in Subic trying to get me to have an objective look at the merry-go-round I was on. He was able to separate things into priorities. He could see the wood from the trees, whereas I could only see each tree, and then only when I got close to it. He suggested an order for our priorities and knew me well enough to be able to grin and say, 'You handle the day-to-day merry-go-round, Jim. Count the pesos. Hear the confessions. Give the *allocutios*. And if the nuns get depressed, give their diddies a lift. You're good at that!

'Meanwhile I'll be the real parish priest. There are big problems here in the Third World which you are only complicating by running around like a red-arsed bee.'

I could do nothing but laugh. That was Seamus.

7

Subic, Zambales
8 May 1974

Dear Annette,

The logic (just dawned on me) of using a large sheet of paper doesn't spring from any wide-ranging ambitions; with a big sheet one can sort of lie on it and not be afraid one's innermost thoughts will be blown out on the plaza by the fan.

Thanks for your letter. No Oriental or Filipino could ever write a letter like that. Here one has to be convoluted and wordy and indirect and unspontaneous, and it drives me daft. Yours was a tonic.

Do I like music? Yes, to sit down purposefully and listen to it. I don't seem to be able to work and listen at the same time. I came out here with two items of luggage – a Jerusalem Bible and a tenor banjo. I have a great feeling for Irish folk music but I play indifferently. I never had a group to practise with.

Recently a *rondalla* group visited me because someone told them I played the banjo and their instruments were stringed too. They asked me to play and I wobbled through a few jigs and reels. The leader, oldish and with only one snaggly tooth left in front, asked could he play my banjo. I told him I'd be delighted. Then he played 'The Black and

White Rag' in a way that rooted me to the ground with my mouth open. I put the banjo back under the bed, determined never to play in public again in a country that has so many virtuosos of string.

I keep a few hidden talents up my sleeve, like being able to drive nails, catch a trout, sole a shoe and enjoy a good book, so that all my illusions, hopefully, will never be shattered simultaneously.

Three books of the lighter sort which I got my hands on recently gripped me in a way Edgar Rice Burroughs or *The Swiss Family Robinson* did as a child: Michener's *The Drifters*, *The Day of the Jackal* and *The Camerons* by Robert Crighton. So you see I'm not so badly off. I even have *De-Schooling Society* and here, above all places, does it tell the truth, because we have all the vices of the American education system and little of the scholarship.

I get the *Tablet*, the *New Yorker* and the *New Internationalist* (all subscribed for me by friends) and therefore I'm moderately schizophrenic on politics and religion.

I'm going home to Ireland later in the year for a vacation and if I have to I'll burn enough boats so that I'll have to come back. Besides preaching the gospel, part of the Columban thing is finance and administration and I'm afraid I might get pressured into home service again now that I have more or less settled down here. It has taken so much out of me to get acculturated to the Philippines and I am very close to being at home here now.

My mother is seventy-seven and insists on living alone in our old thatched house. I have a brother and three sisters over there too – all younger than I. If I am in London

91

I would like to see you and chew the rag with yourself and the children for a while. I've made no plans for a stopover on my way home but I will stay a while with you on my way back in February 1975.

Thank you for the nice words of encouragement. The old-timers here say that when one goes back to Europe after a stint here, brimming over with the joys and hopes and frustrations of a very different kind of existence, the hardest thing to bear is the lack of interest in what goes on out here – particularly on the part of the clergy. The dialogue runs something like this:

'Where are you now, Father? Out foreign somewhere?'

'Yes, Philippines.'

'Very hot out there, they say.'

'Between 80 degrees and 100 degrees in the dry season and during the monsoons, it's – '

'Will you be home for long?'

'Oh, a few months.'

'Have Limerick any chance against Tipp this year in the hurling?'

And so on and so on.

This is unkind and exaggerated, of course, but the truth is that 99 per cent of people are interested only in their own four-by-fours. It's easy for missionaries to think like that too but I find I cannot afford to do so. I believe that the second stage of the Church's mission is about to begin now in a world accelerating in thought, freedom of expression and globalisation. It is very important for me to remain au fait with what's happening in politics, economics and religion in Latin America, Africa and Asia rather than remain tied to the European mother.

The contribution to the missions of a country like England is relatively small but it does offer vital help in another way: It is a watershed for fairly reliable educational and technical services to the Third World, particularly in Africa and Asia. It spearheads stuff like Ban the Bomb, has set up Oxfam, and through the *New Internationalist* emphasises concepts like environmental protection, world hunger, class and racial prejudice in a secular setting, which is a relief from religiosity. Get your hands on a copy of the *New Internationalist*. It's way ahead of the type of pious, hagiographical promotion of mission at home which I've become sick of.

And then there are people like yourself who not only sacrifice for basic needs out here but who want to become involved in the spirit as well as the deed. I thank you for that and while I'm not even remotely expressing the reality of the mission thing as I experience it (so far I'm only training myself to think my way through it) I hope, some day, to be relaxed and detached enough to talk it through with you.

There has been one big change in my life since I wrote last. I now have a partner in the parish and he's ten years younger than I. His name is Seamus Connolly. We were in language school together and came to Zambales together. When I mentioned him to you in some previous letter I made that throwaway remark that he was 'half mad'. I can see it has you bamboozled. I meant it as the finest compliment I can pay to a man.

The conventional person provokes nothing, enlivens nothing. Seeing through the conventional, and going against it to acquire a more creative perspective on life, is madness to the safe man. Yet, deep down, he is envious of it and knows that because of it things will begin to happen around him which will liven up his boring life. It is a quality which means being different but not idiosyncratic, being a hellraiser but not destructive. I'm talking about the meaning of an English word in my culture.

A small farmer in my townland of Brackile would tell a woman he was mad about her when he meant he loved her. Saying a man is half mad is good, while saying he's mad is bad. What I meant about Seamus is that he is so serious about his mission, so interested in its progress, so contemptuous of waffle and convention that he pushes reason and instinct beyond the usual social parameters just to see what will happen, what reaction he'll get among people whose thinking has become stratified, if not ossified. When he does that, people can bristle and he can sometimes bring the roof in on himself. All this means is that, while he has considerable political and public-relations skills, he suddenly decides not to use them. It doesn't mean he's insensitive. It only means he's half mad.

Two acts of pure mischief having nothing to do with evangelisation rebounded on him recently and a third rebounded on me.

He was doing a *Romeo and Juliet* interpretation from the balcony at one of the young Filipina nuns passing by below. He professed undying love dramatically, and obviously realistically, because I was called before Mother Provincial the following day (that was quick) and asked to account for the love affair going on between Seamus and her nun. I laughed because I knew he thought the same sister a bit of a lightweight, and so I explained

Connolly's love of Shakespeare (my ass!) and how the scene could be misinterpreted if some nun, illiterate as far as Shakespeare went, was to be peeping around the wall of the church and was to carry the story home. (Which was what happened.)

I persuaded Seamus to meet Mother Provincial the following day by arrangement with her. He knew she had called me in, and why. When she complimented him on his love of Shakespearean theatre and asked him to recite some passages, he nearly choked.

He got into serious trouble with Judge Affable and had to go through all sorts of hoops to put it right, including taking Judge to San Miguel to play a game of golf. Judge's wife, Viming, knew who to call when a pipe leaked, when the fridge went on the blink or the walls started falling down. She often dropped by but always with either Ludy or Ging or Esther. Seamus started joking with Judge and told him that I would bear watching, that I was a devil for the women. In Ireland, particularly in Dublin, that is called slagging. To the utter surprise of Seamus, Judge took him seriously, went home and had a row with Viming. Then all sorts of *tagapamagitans* (go-betweens) had to be called in to defuse the situation.

Seamus's sense of humour backfired again with Doctor Nepomuceno, who is the husband of Esther. I came back from Batiawan, a farming plateau in the Zambales Mountains, a barrio of the parish which was inaccessible by road and at least twenty miles away. I was there with Posadas for two days and it was raining all the time. Thinking the rain was as good as a wash, I never took a proper shower because there were none, other than the odd waterfall, and only dried myself after each wetting. As a result I got some sort of fungus in the armpits and crotch and an inflammation of the foreskin.

I explained my predicament to Seamus and he said he would go for Nepo. Nepo came with his bag, gave me a dirty look, jabbed penicillin into me and went away.

'That's most unusual for Nepo,' I said.

'Do you know how much penicillin he gave you?' Seamus asked.

'How would I know? The guy didn't even wait to tell me.'

'Jesus, I think I've done it again,' said Seamus. 'I was joking him of course when I told him you had probably dipped your wick on the mountain and got a dose. The bloody man must have believed me. They've no sense of humour whatsoever here!'

'Seamus, they are our close friends but that doesn't mean they understand our brand of humour. Call the *tagapamagitans* again and clear my good name.'

You may find this brand of mischief juvenile, Annette, but I want to tell you something about the kind of priests we are. You only know the public performance of the dressed-up version in your parish in Surbiton or elsewhere. We read our breviary, say our prayers, do the usual stuff priests all over the world do. But, by ourselves, we take the opportunity to let our hair down.

Seamus and I have never been ecclesiastically engineered into performing clerical seals. We value our personalities and identity too much. Of course we go over the top, especially out here, where our roles in society are seen as ritualistic rather than socially dynamic. The level

Third to sixth class, Brackile National School, 1944. Jim is in the front row, second from left.

Jim's ordination photograph, taken in December 1958 by Martin Dempsey, who was to be shot dead in Mindanao in 1970.

The Pioneer pin stayed on Jim's lapel for a further eleven years.

The Kennedy family, 1965. Back row, left to right: Jim, Breda, Harry, Celia and Mary. Seated: Nora, Jim's mother, and Paddy, Jim's father.

Olongapo, 1972. It was a city of hotels, nightclubs, hair salons and brothels, all with one purpose – to capitalise on freely spent American dollars.

The 'Dirty Dozen'. Standing, from left: Nepo, Doc, Seamus, Dr Carlito Lesaca, Jim, Romy Maningding, Mr Lesaca, Mr Soriano and Judge. Seated from left: Esther, Ludy, Ging and Viming.

Mayor Dangal Guevara and Jim, shortly after burying the hatchet over the 'Dulo affair', at a graduation ceremony at Subic Central Elementary School. The peacemaker was the school's principal, left of picture.

Jim saying an outdoor Mass for a group of farmers, flanked by Juanito Posadas and Teddy Bacani (with back to camera).

With Sister Carolyn and the fishermen of Libertador. The Zambales Mountains are visible in the background.

At a screening of the film *Cactus Flower*, on the basketball court of St James High School in 1974. Seated in the front row, from left, are Jim, Seamus and Sister Josefa Aldana.

A day off, spent inland with some students from St James High School.

Philippine Independence Day, 1972. Jim with eight of the youngest teachers in St James High School, three of whom were former students then.

St Vincent's Church, Candelaria, with the tin-roofed *convento* to the right. The church was burnt to the ground in the eighties, after a fire spread from the nearby market. It was rebuilt by Father Fintan Murtagh.

Jim and his trusty Volkswagen in 1972, at a new parish site in the hills south of Olongapo.

Jim with Sister Theresia Ngo (Thu Thuy) in Manila, at her graduation as a nurse in 1972.

Vising, front row, second from left, pictured with student officers from Zambales High School, Iba, Zambales, in 1961. She taught journalism, Filipino and English.

The Benavidez family in 1968: Vising (centre) is dressed as a novice. Also shown are her four brothers and four sisters, her parents and her grandmother.

of isolation from the culture creates a silent, inner frustration, which comes out in colourful language and exaggerated reaction. The energy-sapping heat has something to do with it too. It brings about a mental torpidity in us which is enfeebling, which we feel helpless against and which we lash out at in frustration.

I am actually beginning to suspect, in spite of all my optimism, that Seamus is in the wrong place and in the wrong job in Subic. He has too much to offer which can't get out. He is underused, remarkable though his contribution is, and I have a premonition that he is heading for a destination farther up the banks of the Little Big Horn if he doesn't take a long, hard look at where he's going. I can mullock away . . . I think. No, I'm sure.

No one can exist out here as 'action man', as a revolutionary thinker cutting through swathes of ecclesiastical and cultural blancmange, without treading on people's toes. The price is too high when there are other, more suitable jobs for him in research, development, higher education within the Church.

The problem is that the Columbans are an infantry brigade and they make no distinction between the slogger and the strategist. A guy like Seamus is of great value to our society, which is top-heavy with sloggers and very light on men of thought, those who can scout and plan our future. I've no reason to believe he's appreciated either by his bishop or his superiors for the contribution he's trying to make.

We have developed a comradeship which is good for both of us. He uses me as a sounding post. I respond honestly. (He says honesty is one of the few talents I've got!) When he isolates a practical area for exploration and is convincing in his presentation of it, I go along with it.

Since he came, we've done some things which I'm very happy with, and which have taken the witch-doctor feeling off me. The baptismal ceremony from the text of the Roman Ritual is a bit unrealistic and rather turgid for here. Seamus rewrote the service in Tagalog, aiming at educating parents and sponsors in core Christian values and challenging them to live it. Baptism day is probably the only time we will see most of them. It is a lively, crystal-clear and witty service, and I now have it off pat.

We ran the Marriage Encounter in the parish for our key couples and an abridged version of it in Tagalog as an experiment in one of the barrios. He organised an hour's slot at prime time for himself on local radio once a week during which he takes popular songs (e.g. 'Bridge over Troubled Waters') and interprets them in terms of Christian values. It goes down well.

To finish, just two instances of the Connolly approach, which to me were radical, but to Seamus, normal.

Many of the people in Batiawan had their houses destroyed by the typhoon and the portage of repair materials from Florida Blanca at the bottom of the plateau to the top was extremely difficult with no motorised transport. In his time, Ned McKenna had a small barrio chapel built there. It was just galvanised sheets – top and sides. It had no altar, nor seats, was without a hanging door and had an earthen floor. It was more of a symbol of worship than a place of worship and had been used for services perhaps once or twice. The solution of Seamus was, 'Strip it down and divide it up so that the people will have roofs over their heads.'

'What if McKenna had it consecrated?' I asked.

'Voodoo, James, voodoo,' answered Seamus.

It was the perfect solution, but it would have never occurred to me. Too many attitudes of the pre-Vatican II Church were still ingrained in me. One evening we were sitting on the veranda sipping our San Miguels or gin and lime as the sun went down. Father Pedro de la Rosa was pottering around in front of his Aglipayan church. There was no doubt about it; he was very poor. His soutane – he insisted on wearing black, whereas we wore white – was old and shiny. His children weren't well dressed. The attitude of some Columban priests would have been, 'Serves him right, the bloody heretic.'

Zambales was considered an Aglipayan province when the Columbans arrived in 1950. In the twenty years up to the seventies, there was a lot of cut and thrust between the two Churches, the Roman one winning out because of its schools and the money it ploughed into parishes. In fairness, reactionary and all as it was, ours was less antediluvian, theologically – and that's saying something.

'We've taken away all his parishioners,' Seamus said, 'his means of support. I think we should contribute to his upkeep.'

It seemed reasonable and ecumenical and we did it, but didn't let Conrado, our fiscal, know, nor any of the Columbans. If they ever found out, we would be in serious trouble. There was a thing in canon law called *co-operatio in diviniis* for which there were instant penalties. Supporting a schismatic on a long-term basis would have been top of the list.

I'm sorry to have focused on your question about Seamus, but I think you should know more about the nitty-gritty of our lives, rather than general *ráiméis*. Next time I promise to present a wider picture, and some *ráiméis* for dessert.

8

I never thought of the priesthood as a job in the same way as civil servants and teachers think of their professions as jobs. What I had was more of a state of mind. I saw myself as a sort of prophet, ready to prophesy like Amos, if our civilisation began to go seriously askew. I thought I should be a leaven in society – steering it towards fair play for everyone – and having an obligation to deliver a kick up the transom in some shape or form to those who wilfully, and without repentance, abused the principle of fair play. I was not into ambition, manipulation or the politics of 'getting on'. Then, these were just not important to me, and still aren't.

I never gave any thought, therefore, to the accumulation of money normally associated with jobs. Living hand-to-mouth suited me, as long as I had enough for expenses like cigarettes and razor blades. The beer went on the parish bill under food.

I had never owned a car until six months after arriving in Subic. I got a Volkswagen direct from Germany, and duty-free under some scheme or other. My family paid for it.

The Society looked after my medical bills and gave me a modest handout for a two-week vacation every year. Once a year, I provided an account of my stewardship of parish and school when the books were examined by Tommy Fay, the diocesan finance man. The progress (or lack of it) in the finances of the parish or school was easy to measure. The problem was how to measure the extension I was building to the Kingdom of God in Subic.

On the theory that what you don't know won't trouble you, I concentrated on the problems of this life, because I could not make any fist at all of the next, beyond trying to believe it existed and accepting that others had faith in its existence.

In the same way that the people of Brackile, my home townland in Pallasgrean, County Limerick, would say about some neighbour having 'a big job up in Dublin', it dawned on me that, besides being a prophet in waiting, I had the first big job of my life in Subic. I was almost forty and, for my mother's sake at least, I would make a go of it.

So it was inevitable that I never took Doc Novales' advice to work out a programme of radical action on this so-called mountain of his. It was the hallmark of our crowd in Brackile to face each day as it came and to be happy to have some reason or another to justify getting up for the next. I was acutely aware, though, of the contradiction between the fire-fighting approach to evangelisation and the long term. A barrio Mass one Saturday evening in Calapandayan was a case in point.

I walked out of it in a huff, because most of my congregation had drifted to the small plaza across the road to watch a beauty contest. I couldn't hear myself with the music and then the cheers and yells as each contestant mounted the stage and took her place in the line. I could see it all – twenty yards away, across the road – through the big front door of the church, which was left open for ventilation during Mass.

Had I known then that the 'beauties' were all transvestites, I probably would have put on my Celtic Jesus act, which is a Jesus of anger, irreconcilable, culturally, with the Jesus of harmony and *bahala na*, the Filipino Jesus.

So, like a Filipino Jesus, I just reproached my good friends, Elizabeth Molina and Priscilla Embate, teachers in St James High, who had been to Mass that evening, with the question, 'Why did you let me get egg on my face?'

They had no idea what I was talking about. I explained that even though it was a fund-raiser for the mayor, some of the contestants were pimps from Olongapo. They should have warned me in advance and I would have rescheduled the Mass so as not to be outmanoeuvred by a transvestite beauty contest.

'I could not tell you what to do,' Elisabeth said. 'You are the parish priest and the director of St James High School.'

What she was saying to me was that it wasn't part of her culture to advise me, her superior, and secondly, it was part of her culture to have no problem at all with transvestites and beauty contests of the male kind. Yet she wasn't saying, 'It's your hard luck, Father!' There was some cultural tangle in there that prevented direct dialogue and understanding, and I'd have to get to grips with it.

Calapandayan, Filipinised from the Spanish 'street of the blacksmith', was a middle-class area south of the town. The mayor, Dangal Guevara, lived there in a modest concrete house. A few hundred yards further south, at the end of Calapandayan, or Dulo (meaning end), as it was known, was a cluster of about twenty clubs, which had a reputation among US Marines as being the worst in Asia. It attracted the tough chaws, the kinky-sex merchants and those who wanted to stay out of sight of the Military Police while on shore leave. The area was so tactless in advertising its wares that it had one roadside club called the Foreskin Inn.

The mayor turned a blind eye to its excesses because it brought dollars into the municipality. It was an embarrassment to the likes of Priscilla and Elisabeth, and raucous scenes of familiarity between the hostesses and the sailors on the balconies of the clubs, as travellers passed by on Victory Liner buses, was very shameful in the Filipino culture. The Filipino population of Subic learned to live with it, to pretend it didn't exist. I didn't and couldn't because I knew what went on there from Marines I had met. And I was Irish, of course.

For the meantime though, a few score fornications a day among consenting adults in Dulo wasn't going to unbalance civilisation – even for an Irish Catholic – but there were limits, as I found out the hard way some time later.

Before we had a chance to begin work on prioritised strategies for pre-evangelisation in Subic, Seamus and I got catapulted into a row with the mayor which we hadn't planned and didn't want.

Dangal Guevara, the mayor, was a nice man. He wasn't a practising Catholic, but spent a lot of time in church as a *ninong* at baptisms and weddings. When two boys out of second year in St James got the clap in Dulo, I mentioned to Dangal that the hygiene regulations there mustn't be so hot, and would he do something about it. (Incidentally, one of the boys admitted his father had paid for this, his first experience.) Dr Nepo had also complained about a child which he brought into the world with syphilis of the eyes a few months previously, but nothing was done about that, either.

It began on a Friday afternoon when a young lady came in a hurry to the *convento*, spoke to Tony, the cook, and asked to see one of the nuns. Tony pointed her in the direction of the convent, secluded behind the school. Two hours later, Sister Margaret, St James's young, intelligent and buxom Filipina principal, came up to the *sala* and without any beating about the bush said to me, 'I've just heard a story and it's the worst I've ever heard. I find it hard to think that we're not, one way or another, involved in it.'

The girl, one of the hostesses from Dulo Calapandayan, had walked the mile to St James with blood running down her thighs. She didn't even have jeepney fare. She said that an American sailor, instead of having normal sex, made her copulate with a Coke bottle while he masturbated. The Coke bottle injured her cervix and Dr Nepo was now taking care of her.

This was only the tip of the iceberg. The stories of oppression and enslavement by the *amo* (the employer – the madam – usually a middle-aged Filipina) which the girls in some of the clubs had to endure were horrifying. This was the first time anyone from inside the strip revealed what went on. Fear of retaliation prevented news getting out.

Seamus and myself discussed it, and with Sister Margaret, called in the 'reliables' and their wives. Sister Margaret went over it with them again.

Martial law, declared by President Marcos in 1972, was in its second year. Its stated objective was to save the Republic from Communism and form a disciplined 'New Society'. I must admit I had welcomed it because the law-and-order situation had gone to the dogs. Jose Maria Sison, who founded the KM (Nationalist Youth Movement, which played a revolutionary role in society like Mao's Red Guards in China), reorganised the old Communist Party in 1968 and renamed its military arm the NPA (New People's Army). The effect of this, added to the general lawlessness, was that between the autumn of

1971 and the autumn of 1972 hand grenades were thrown at a Liberal Party rally in Metro Manila; a merchant ship, the MV *Caragatan*, was seized and discovered to be carrying a shipment of firearms for the NPA; and bombs continued to rock the capital.

Martial law was well received at first. It resulted in a dramatic reduction in crime, violence and the use of guns. Urban streets were safer. Apart from that there was little sign of a 'New Society'. Suppression had brought a temporary quiet. What came with it was inevitable: rule by decree; the suspension of habeas corpus, freedom of the press, freedom of speech and the right to assembly; the imposition of strict censorship; and a midnight-to-4 AM curfew.

We decided at the meeting to put the New Society to the test. Local law, which was in the hands of the local politicians, would have been little use anyway. There was no way we could ever ask the victim to testify in court, and there was no way she would ever agree, knowing what the consequences were likely to be.

The front-page headlines, one week later, in a national Sunday newspaper – one of the few still in business after the introduction of martial law – read BLITZKRIEG IN ZAMBALES: ARMY CLOSES DOWN SLEAZY NIGHTCLUBS. We had got action on a scale bigger and far quicker than we expected.

The municipal-government officials in Subic were in a spin. They had watched it all happen. If the mayor – who was small fry in the province – was in a spin, there was consternation in Iba. The governor, the political (but now toothless) head of the province, felt undermined, but not half as badly as the provincial head of the PC (Philippine Constabulary), a colonel whose job it was to push the reforms of the New Society, measure its progress by hunting down communist insurgents, enforce the decrees of Marcos and make sure the curfew was observed.

The 'blitzkrieg' was the biggest shock of all to the colonel because it took place in his bailiwick, unknown to him. A few truckloads of well-armed military from Manila blocked off the Dulo strip at both ends, searched it for arms and drugs (finding little) and put up closed-for-business notices on the clubs. They then returned to Manila, without as much as saying hello. That was ominous in a Philippine context.

It took no time before the original complaint was traced back to St James through the military grapevine. The colonel, embarrassed at being caught with his pants down, went to the ecclesiastical head of the province, our bishop, Harry, and said how shamed he was by all this. This shame, which is *hiya*, can be used as a first-class weapon in interpersonal relations and therefore in getting a message across. Harry knew exactly what it meant.

He summoned his Vicar General, Joe Conneely, drove south with him to Subic, woke up Seamus and myself from siesta and asked us what were we up to. They neither praised nor blamed us, backed nor disowned us. The prevailing emotion on their faces was agitation that we had stirred up a hornets' nest. Anyone with any knowledge of the workings of the Church will give you a hundred to one that bishops hate hornets' nests.

'Did their stealthy arrival,' Seamus asked, after they had left, 'mean that we are too much of an embarrassment to be visited while people are awake?' Seamus loved to round off the picture.

The mayor, being a nice man, and a philosophical one too, sat tight for a while, and then things began to happen in Subic.

I was warned by a cousin of Conrado, Steve Custodio of Baloy Beach, not to travel alone at night, that I would be shot – such was the anger and the language of the club owners. I treated it as Filipino melodrama. The mayor, who paid the tuition of forty St James students (whom he considered deserving) in a scheme known as the Mayor's Scholarships, cancelled his payments. That caused great distress to the parents of the students concerned, and would have to be addressed.

The town was split (at a guess I'd say 10 per cent for us, 40 per cent for the mayor and 50 per cent uninvolved) but, like Harry Byrne, all were uncomfortable with the tension and confrontation. Seamus and myself got the runs. I got away first, for two days – my runs being new and therefore the worse, while those of Seamus were familiar territory to him.

When I returned, Seamus was just being released from the municipal jail at the intervention of a lieutenant of the local PC, who told the mayor's municipal police to cop themselves on. He was one smart soldier. Seamus had been arrested for rumour-mongering, a crime under martial law. As they were leaving the *municipio*, the lieutenant, with a twinkle in his eye, asked Seamus, 'What do you have to say about these rumour-mongering charges, anyway?'

'What I mongered,' Seamus said, glaring at the local police chief, 'was not rumour but fact. Dulo was a cesspool because the club owners and the mayor wouldn't get their acts together. If they had, everything would still be bright and breezy, as it is in Olongapo – you know, the beer, the craic, the missionary position and keep the change, ma'am.' The lieutenant smiled broadly, but the local gendarmes didn't think it a bit funny.

We handled the scholarship issue by holding a general

meeting in the school auditorium to explain events and the issues behind them. We confiscated a tape recorder from one of the mayor's henchmen, who had been sent to carry back a report.

'The bowsie can carry it back in his head, like the rest of them,' Seamus – who was spin-doctoring the operation – whispered to me.

Paz Esquivel, one of the teachers, made her name that day. Why she was MC, I can't remember, but she proved why she was an ex-nun (from the same congregation that ran the school) rather than a nun. In Philippines, nuns aren't supposed to be firebrands or put themselves in danger, but she took the meeting by the scruff of the neck, outlined the role of the school in Subic with clarity and conviction, lambasted the forces that were eroding its moral and educational values and called on me, the director of the school, to make the speech of the day.

I didn't make one. I didn't have to. Paz had made it. I asked the packed audience to dwell on what she had said and assured the parents that the school would carry the cost of the scholarships until every student had graduated. I had no idea how we would do it, but we had to.

Paz was offered the principalship of a Columban-run high school in Mabayon, Olongapo the following year, and accepted. I wasn't asked by the Columban parish priest there whether he could talk to Paz before making his offer. She just disappeared during the school holidays. She also deserved the promotion.

I wrote, in the meeting's aftermath, to the head chaplain of Subic's naval base, asking him to pass around the hat among the chaplains, to help bail us out, seeing that it was the human tool of Uncle Sam that got us into the mess in the first place.

I never got an answer.

Seamus and myself were at the Tuesday-evening dinner in Columban parish, Olongapo, a week later. Ned McKenna was in charge there then. He had maintained a studied but far from passionate interest in our difficulties, and it got up the nose of Seamus.

'Ned, did you know when you agreed to the mayor's scholarship scheme during your time at Subic that the money was coming from fornications in Dulo?' he asked. 'And how did you feel when you were counting it?' Not waiting for a reply, he added (for the benefit of all the guys at table), 'And why didn't we get more support from you guys?'

'I didn't think that you, knowing as much as you do, needed any support from anyone,' replied Ned on his way into the kitchen.

'Spoken like a true twenty-year man!' shouted Seamus after him.

'Let's go home, Seamus,' I said, 'before you get me into more trouble.'

The case history of the Dulo affair explained Philippine culture and sociology to Seamus and myself in a way we could never have understood had we not gone through it.

First of all, action could never have been taken about Dulo had we not got the right channels to the top. In this case, we had grade-A *palakasan* (influence). Ludy's brother, Bishop Mariano Gaviola, later Archbishop of Lipa, acted as liaison for the hierarchy with the Marcos government. He was on good terms with the defence minister, Juan Ponce Enrile, and with the head of the army, Fidel Ramos. Enrile, we heard afterwards, asked Mariano whether this was a genuine complaint or just another whinge from the Church. Mariano, who had our letter with him, showed it to Enrile, who acted immediately.

The identity of the Dirty Dozen, the name by which we became known in Subic, was made public. With Seamus and myself, they were Doc and Ging Novales, Ging's father, Mr Soriano, Dr Carlito Lesaca, the son of Mrs Lesaca, Judge and Viming Affable, Dr and Esther Nepumoceno, the Tapias, Ludy and Ric, and Romy Maningding. They were brave and never flinched in their loyalty to us or to their own people.

The 'on-the-fence' attitude of the townspeople had many explanations.

1. Seamus and I were foreigners, therefore it was our problem.
2. Confrontation on public issues rarely happens in Philippines unless through a constitutionally established group which tribalises the individual, giving him or her official safety in numbers.
3. The mayor was a popular man. Many people had *utang na loob* (a debt owed for favours) to him, first as *ninong*, and then for political favours. Municipal employees and those connected with them couldn't side against him.
4. The Church was not generally seen as having a role to play in social change.
5. Right and wrong had little to do with the incident once it became a confrontation. Then all that mattered was *pakikisama*, *hiya* and *kanya kanya* (sticking together, shame and every man for himself).
6. If the bishop kept his head down during the affair, why should parishioners stick their necks out?
7. Fear of authority.

The estrangement between the mayor and myself lasted for a year and caused headaches for many programme organisers in the municipality. If he was there, I couldn't attend. If I had a major role in some programme, he wouldn't go. It ended at a graduation ceremony in the Central Elementary School. The principal, a formidable Ilocana, invited us both. On our way out we shook hands and the town breathed a sigh of relief. Harmony, one of the most important words in the Asian vocabulary, was restored.

The girl from Dulo who started it all had been forgotten once the closed-for-business signs had gone up in the clubs – which, incidentally, reopened a month later.

What pisses me off now, twenty-five years later, is that I forgot all about her then – and I was supposed to be in the Jesus business.

I do believe I would not forget about her now.

The first time I met Doming Maneses, I tripped over him in the dark. He was asleep on the floor of the *sala* in the *convento* with five other barrio men from Batiawan who had come down to Mayor Guevara for help. I had got back from somewhere near midnight and the electricity was off again because of a typhoon. We lit candles and he introduced me to his friends.

The people of Batiawan, which is in the municipality of Subic, never voted in municipal elections – they were too far away.

Batiawan was at the sharp end of a mountainous isosceles triangle of land which speared inland, beginning at Subic on the South China Sea, running for eight miles across the roadless Zambales Mountains, and ending overlooking the town of Florida Blanca in Pampanga, a flat rice-land and sugar-growing

112

province. It would never have been populated, I was told, except for President Magsaysay (born in Iba and killed in an air crash in 1957) who used it to solve a political problem. The Huks, who were Communist guerrillas, fought side by side with the Americans during World War II. They were few enough, nationwide, then, but were thick on the ground in Zambales, Tarlac and Pampanga. While they were fighting the Japanese, they were acceptable, but after the war they posed the usual problems.

When independence was granted by the Americans to the Philippines in 1946, they became Magsaysay's problem. He solved it by allocating land on the plateau to the guerrillas so that they would lay down their guns and follow the plough. A small number did. Batiawan, a Pampango word for 'view', then developed a reputation for being a troublesome area. To my knowledge, no mayor of Subic ever ventured up there. Dangal, being a practical politician, knew there were no votes there, and so he sent Doming and his delegation on to me.

Typhoon damage had created hunger and homelessness there and, after I had given them as much rations as I had, they insisted that I go up there to see for myself. That was when Posadas and I set out with them, and when I contracted the unmentionable disease, disclosed by Seamus to Nepo.

Doming Maneses was an unusual man. You couldn't but like him. He had been a student leader during the pre-martial-law tensions in Manila. With a known credibility among the older ex-Huks, he got a piece of land in Batiawan and lived there with his wife, child and a very familiar-looking animal, which he called a fig. Some Filipinos, and Doming was one of them, interchange 'P's and 'F's with impartiality.

Because he was college-educated and spoke excellent

113

English, he led whatever delegations had to be led outside of the plateau.

Within the plateau, some of the old campaigners ruled the roost. It was Doming who told me what happened to the galvanised sheets stripped from Ned McKenna's chapel. The barrio *capitan*, an old campaigner, appropriated them for himself and his mates, leaving the neediest people roofless. I talked for a long time with Doming while I was on the plateau during the rain, and promised him, like MacArthur, that I would try to come back for the fiesta after Easter.

9

The Holy Week ceremonies had come and gone; we were in an Easter Week lull and the thought of going to Baguio or Manila for the guts of a week appeared not only attractive, but downright possible – even deserving.

Seamus had seen the *flagelantes* for the first time and it was the talking point of his first Holy Week in Subic. I had known they'd be coming around 11 AM on Good Friday, and as they came up the street and into the church, I called Seamus, who was finalising his radio programme in his room.

The *flagelantes*, as a Holy Week phenomenon, was local to Castillejos, Subic and Olongapo. Castillejos is the site of the Balaybay Calvary on Good Friday, where penitents drag wooden crosses to a hilltop, accompanied by the *flagelantes*. I've heard reports that some mild form of crucifixion often took place there, but I never witnessed it, being too busy with ceremonies myself.

The *flagelantes* are mostly young men, usually up to twenty of them in a group, who walk in procession through the town, each one flailing himself on the back with a small whip. The exercise is meant to be expiation for sin usually arising from a 'sacred promise' made during the year to do penance for something they feel guilty about.

We watched them approach. They wore nothing but pants. Their faces were covered in black bandannas to mask their identities. Vines of greenery were twisted around their legs and woven around their heads like a crown of thorns. Behind them was an old woman, driving them on as one would drive cattle.

'Holy Jesus!' Seamus said. 'Would you look at all the blood on their backs!'

The whips weren't cutting deep, but they were spreading the blood, probably made by light razor-blade cuts before the men set out. When they disappeared into the church, I said, 'They're looking for a blessing, Seamus. How about it?'

'You must be joking,' he snorted. 'That's nothing but public exhibitionism, and sick stuff at that. I wouldn't give their performance an ounce of credibility by being seen in the same church as them.'

'Come down anyway, just as a spectator. Pretend you're an ethnologist and this is a new cultural experience. You can stand at the side door if it makes you that sick.'

The *flagelantes* were lying face-down on the floor in front of the altar, with their arms outstretched. I talked to the old woman, getting into the same argument and reaching the same conclusion as the year before: there would be no blessing but I wouldn't interfere if each one of them wanted to reconcile themselves silently with God. I told her to tell them that and then I took their photos again.

'You're some operator,' Seamus said, and with some distaste added, 'Some day you may even make bishop.'

Seamus, the post-Vatican II man, wouldn't have believed that religious masochism wasn't the monopoly of Filipino young men only. Fifty years before, some of the earlier Columbans wore hair shirts, and some of the Filipina nuns recruited early on by newly arrived European orders had had to put sticks into their corsets to make them stay erect. This was done under

116

the direction of the European nuns from Spain and France, who also insisted that their Filipina nuns shower but once a week and wear silk stockings – in the tropics!

When I mentioned the upcoming fiesta in Batiawan to Seamus, he jumped at it. It would be a bit of excitement – more than if we went to Baguio or Manila. It would be totally different from Subic, and would be a bit cooler up there.

In no time, we had a team organised: three of the parish nuns, in case there were children to be prepared for First Communion; Nepo for medicine; Posadas for agriculture; and Father Teodoro Bacani, a bright young Filipino priest who was in charge of the CCP (Christian Communities Programme) in the diocese and was doing a brilliant job at it. He was a native of Pampanga and spoke the dialect, Pampango, which would come in useful with some of the people up there.

We borrowed a four-wheel-drive truck, which Seamus insisted on driving. It took us two hours the roundabout way to reach Florida Blanca, where we began the ascent to Batiawan. Going up the escarpment without benefit of a road from the base to the plateau was scary. Some of the inclines were over 45 degrees and there were times I thought the truck might somersault backwards. The steeper the path got, the more Seamus loved it, and eventually he got us there.

The dust of the clay plaza had no sooner settled after our grand arrival than it was redistributed by the arrival of a small maroon Ford, with battered sides, that came skidding to a stop.

Out stepped a tall 'film star' of a Filipina in short skirt, high leather boots and two-inch-diameter earrings. She was as good-looking as Jane Russell or Rita Hayworth. And she had driven up the escarpment by herself. She had come, she said, for the wedding of her half-brother, and it was a great tribute to her father and Batiawan that I had come to do it. It was the first I heard of a wedding, but then I was in a place unconnected by road to the outer world, and the message which I should have got earlier in Subic had, of course, got lost in transit.

'*Ganyan ang buhay* (That's life), isn't it Father?'

'*Ganyan, talaga* (It is indeed),' says I.

'And you will not forget to be in our house tomorrow around midday so that the celebrations can begin? It's over the next hill, down in the ravine. Doming will show you.'

Doming gave us a great welcome and, introducing him to our team, I deliberately treated him as the barrio *capitan*. I was still very vexed that the other fellow should have exploited the galvanised-sheets situation for himself and his pals, so vexed that I couldn't conceal it. I utterly despise cute hoors, 'smart men', conmen, stroke-pullers, exploiters, cheaters, manipulators, back-slappers, ingratiators. If I had to rewrite the Ten Commandments – and I often felt like doing it – I'd reduce them to one, incorporating all of the above.

I couldn't wait to ask Doming: 'Who is the beautiful woman with the flashing eyes and the big earrings?'

'Long story,' he answered, 'but for the moment I'll just tell you that she is now a widow, was a well-known night-club singer and is the daughter by the first marriage of Lolo Pedring, the "patriarch" of Batiawan and a former mayor of Florida Blanca, whom you will meet tomorrow. It is his son by the third wife who is getting married.'

Batiawan is not a proper plateau in the sense that its terrain is not flat tableland on top. It is a series of rolling hills and ravines, about a mile square. Clearly visible to the north-west is Pinatubo, a volcanic mountain, and the highest in Zambales at 1,780 metres.

Like many place names in Irish which accurately describe a locality, Pinatubo, roughly translated, means 'a good place to grow things'. Volcanic ash, after an eruption in the 1500s, had obviously made the surroundings fertile. The Aetas, a dark-skinned and very small-statured people indigenous to Zambales, called it a sacred mountain and still lived in the mountain territory (some of it surviving as rainforest) around it and to the north and south of it.

Little did anyone expect then that the volcano would erupt again within twenty years (in 1991), with devastating consequences. One hundred villages were buried and nine hundred people were killed, many of whom were Aetas. Weeks before the eruption, the Aetas knew something was brewing on their mountain. They spoke about smelling sulphur emanating from cracks in the caves in which they sheltered during hunting trips. One such group of hunters was found dead in a cave when the eruptions were over.

There is a lake now in the crater, which is four hundred metres deep and two kilometres in diameter. The lahar flows (a mixture of volcanic ash and water) during the rainy seasons are less threatening, but the new lake, high on the mountain, remains a Sword of Damocles if the crater walls are not up to the job of containment.

Less than ten miles away, Batiawan survived the devastation untouched, by some freak of nature and the elements.

The three priests shared sleeping quarters in a four-metre-square *bahay kubo* with the three Filipino nuns. The nuns were carefully screened off from us, of course. Posadas and Dr Nepo

119

were quartered out among the people like Caesar's soldiers.

Seamus and myself had a bottle of Scotch, which we kept hidden from the nuns – not that they'd drink it, just that priests, nuns and whisky in a *bahay kubo*, on top of an isolated mountain, didn't seem a great idea at the time. When I think back now, thirty years later, three things about those two days on the plateau are crystal clear to me: I got a jolt from the past which caused tears to flow down my face, I ran into the biggest canon-law problem I ever encountered, and I got hypnotised.

Because of the varied, privately owned and people-friendly transport system in the Philippines, its citizens never walk if they can hitch a ride. And so it was that, at the instigation of the nuns, Seamus started up the truck the following morning to go to the wedding site at Lolo Pedring's. The nuns didn't want to get *amorseko* (a very prickly hayseed) on their habits, walking through the cogon grass. Pedring's place was less than a mile and a few ravines away from the level mud plaza of the barrio centre, where Ned McKenna's galvanised chapel once stood.

Halfway there I got off the truck, plain scared that we'd topple over at one mile per hour. It was then I heard the music coming from below. The truck had disappeared round a bend, and the music, although faint, had become clearer. Here on an isolated mountain in Zambales, without electricity or battery radio, I was listening to the voice of Delia Murphy on a wind-up gramophone, singing 'If I Were a Blackbird'. It triggered memories of Brackile and us, as kids, playing the song on our gramophone in the forties, because it was among my father's favourites. It evoked sad feelings – he had died and was buried without me. I had to sit down for a long time to get a grip on myself.

The widow in the flashy earrings, the daughter of Pedring

who brought the gramophone to Batiawan, turned out to be Carmen Guerrero O'Brien. Her husband, an Irish-American, was killed in 1970 flying his small plane over Pangasinan while taking aerial photos for oil geologists. She had been forewarned that Seamus and I were Irish, and brought her late husband's gramophone and collection of 78s. It was the most unlikely and emotive of intrusions given the primitive and Asiatic setting.

The series of bamboo houses that comprised the compound of Pedring were built on a ledge on the side of a wide ravine. They were an architectural wonder of craftsmanship and practicality, and totally unlike any other houses on the plateau. What captivated me was the water running everywhere through bamboo pipes. Carmen, *mirabile dictu,* even had a crate of dry sherry cooling under the spray of water from a perforated section of one bamboo. It tasted wonderful, even though Seamus and myself weren't dry-sherry types.

The morning was lengthening and I was having trouble getting the young couple together to brief them on the marriage ceremony, because I heard the bride-to-be was unwell. Then I saw Nepo going into a room with his doctor's bag.

'She's bleeding,' he said on coming out. 'Most likely she's losing a baby. Give her time to rest and we'll be able to proceed. By the way, did you know she's a Muslim from Mindanao?'

'What!' says I.

'They met in college in Manila and eloped to here. Her people are going to be very angry.'

'Oh shit,' says I.

When I told Seamus and Teddy that we had a canonical problem, they stood back and grinned. We had this Irish slagging going among us, and the Filipinos couldn't understand it at all. Teddy was an exception because he got used to it among the Irish in Rome while he was studying for a Licentiate in Canon Law.

'We don't have a canonical problem,' Seamus replied. 'You have a canonical problem because you're the parish priest.' Teddy, who is now a bishop in Manila, agreed, and with smiling eyes concurred that it was up to me to make serious decisions.

All this canon-law stuff about mixed marriages and dispensations seemed as out of place in the circumstances as Delia Murphy and her blackbird song. I would take a short cut through all the problems and do the marriage as a civil ceremony. The couple were solid lovers with a child on the way, and anyway, true love transcended the boundaries of race and religion. The fiesta Mass for the people would be the religious element, rather than a nuptial Mass.

'Are you legally entitled to do a civil marriage in this country?' Seamus asked, rubbing it in a bit more.

'Calm down,' I said. 'I'm now the captain of a ship in the middle of the Zambales Mountains. You can be the parish priest of Subic until we get down out of here. I'll marry whoever I like.'

Canon law was always my worst suit in the seminary. The late Joe Flynn, DD, DCL, professor of canon law and moral theology in Dalgan, would have expected the political rather than a canonical solution from me. When I had to have faculties to hear Confessions in Meath diocese in the mid-sixties, Joe was my designated examiner, to check that I was compos mentis in canon law. I failed to answer a single question. In despair he said, 'You're too far gone now to do anything about it. I think we have time for nine holes before supper.'

There were no clocks in Batiawan. No one was in a rush – not even myself, a notorious rusher. Lolo Pedring had agreed to do a reading from the Tagalog Bible and was practising it with the help of a grandchild. Doming pointed to a hilltop two hundred metres away. 'The Mass and wedding will take place up there, Father.'

Eventually we got going in a procession that slowly snaked its way to the top. The bride-to-be seemed to have recovered as a result of Nepo's ministrations. We passed through an elaborate archway of bamboo and palm fronds, and on the archway, in foot-high letters, was the pleasant message: WELCOME FATHER KENNEDY AND FRIENDS.

They had put an awful lot of work into the preparations and I felt happy that I hadn't made a meal out of the ecclesiastical-impediments issue. A square *palapala* (bamboo poles with a palm-frond and banana-leaf roof) had been constructed on the summit to keep out the scorching sun, and at the dead centre of the square was a flat-topped rock the size of a small car.

Pedring's patriarchal mien gave a prophetic quality to the words of the Bible, the rock added an Old Testament flavour, the sisters led a willing chorus of popular hymns, and having strolled through the ceremonies, we were on our way down to Pedring's for lunch in an hour and a half. I couldn't remember when I felt so smug after a ceremony.

It was back to the plaza before nightfall for the *sayaw* or festival dance. There was a bonfire going, and the gramophone was playing Filipino folk songs and dance music. Seamus, Teddy and I asked the nuns for a dance but all three refused. We danced with the local women anyway, until we got tired. Nepo was settled down for the night on an orange box, smoking his

123

pipe, when Seamus said to me, 'Anything left in the bottle?'

'Half-full,' I answered.

'Let's go. This dancing under a tropical moon is wearing me out.'

We pleaded tiredness, and as we were saying our goodnights, Sister Florence said she was also tired and asked could she come with us. When she mentioned she hadn't slept the night before, Seamus suggested he had a cure.

'Pills?' she asked.

'No. Hypnotism.'

Seamus was always doing something to broaden his horizons, and a course on hypnotism in Manila had given him some practice. I encouraged Florence to chance it and she agreed, but only on the condition that I was present.

'See, Seamus,' I said, 'the women don't trust you, so I'll be watching you like a hawk.'

He told her to lie down on the *banig* (a plant-fibre mat), her head on a pillow. I was to one side, on my haunches. There were no tables and chairs in this dwelling. Then he started his rigmarole: 'Close your eyes, relax, relax, relax all muscles. Just listen to my voice, to nothing else but my voice . . .'

He went on and on in a drone, and the next thing I knew was that I woke up and Florence was gone.

'Where's Florence gone?' I asked. 'And did you hypnotise her?'

'She's gone to her quarters, and I might as well have been trying to hypnotise that big rock you said Mass on today. But I hypnotised you,' he guffawed with a loud belly laugh.

'I was just taking forty winks after an eventful day, young man,' I answered.

We poured ourselves generous whiskies and then the face of Juanito Posadas was at the opening that served as a window and he was saying to me, 'Come quick, young Pauli has broken his leg dancing.'

For the second time in Batiawan I said, 'Oh, shit.'

Eduardo Pauli, an Aeta, had been hospitalised in the US naval base in Olongapo after he and two others from Batiawan suffered multiple bone fractures in a landslide. In appearance, he could have passed for an authentic miniature of Muhammad Ali, then in his prime. Our friendship had gone back to that hospitalisation, a year previously. Pauli was a little gamecock and kept the hospital staff and patients in good humour while he was recovering. On his discharge, I told him I would take him to Florida Blanca. The doctor told me to emphasise to him in Tagalog and English that he was not to climb trees because he had brittle bones. And now the little gamecock had done it again.

In the end, he wouldn't let me take him to Florida Blanca. Two miles south of Olongapo, on a zigzag road forested on both sides, he asked me to let him out.

'I will be home sooner this way,' he said. 'I know the way.'

I let him off, because his people had no use for roads for thousands of years. He knew the tracks and the mountains and the nature of things in a way the modern Filipino never could or ever will.

When we got up to the bonfire, Nepo, with his pipe still steaming, was putting splints on Pauli's shin. The orange box had come in handy. An old woman was hovering in the background and when I suggested that he should go back with us to the base hospital, she came forward and said, 'I am an old woman living alone and he has lived with me since after the landslide in which his family died. I would not like to lose him again. I will look after him.'

I hadn't known about Pauli's family until then. I looked at Nepo and he nodded. I haven't heard a thing about him or Doming or the lady with the flashing earrings since; nor does it really matter. For a short while I had great communication with them. That's what makes it all worthwhile now.

Shortly after our trip to Batiawan, Seamus went home to Ireland because his father had become seriously ill. After his death, Seamus decided to further his education in Third World economics at Swansea University. He felt that unless he took the initiative himself, none of his superiors would. He didn't reach agreement with the Superior General about it, got his MA off his own bat anyway, and took a job as field director in the Yemen for Concern. The Society had no use for him. He married Evelyn there in 1977. Since then, he has taken a doctorate at Fordham and has maintained his links with the Third World by holding two senior-management posts in Latin America with multi-national corporations.

Some guys go out with a bang.

Brian Williams succeeded Seamus as my parish partner in Subic, and we worked together for less than a year before I completed my term there. He was a young Australian and his purpose in Philippines was to get a fix on the realities of mission work for a year or two before going on to Rome to do postgraduate studies in theology. His ultimate ambition was to teach in one of the Columban seminaries. Brian integrated into the Filipino swing of things with visible success – as most young Australians could. He never talked much about himself or his aspirations, unlike Seamus. Then one day he gave me a paper to sign.

He had fallen in love with an Olongapo girl, a teacher, and he was going to marry her. I knew nothing about it. He needed the signature of a priest in good standing to testify that he was of sound mind. I signed it in a daze.

And then it was time for me to go home to Ireland for a six-month vacation.

10

Dalgan Park, Navan, Ireland
11 November 1974

Dear Annette,

I was wondering about you, but fully confident that I'd hear from you some time.

It's funny that you too should have the wish to respond with nothing less than a great letter – and rarely getting around to it because the ambition is not often matched by the time or the mood. In the last six weeks I've had the first vacation of my life and never felt happier, freer or more relaxed.

The East did wonders for me. I felt it first in Abu Dhabi, where up to three hundred fretful passengers on our 747 had to wait twenty-four hours for Air France to make up its mind whether one of the engines would be fixed or a substitute flown in from Paris. Even the imperturbable Japanese and Indians were fidgety, whereas, after four years in never-never land, the newly metamorphosed Kennedy threw his jacket on the marble floor and promptly fell asleep, not caring if the engine ever got fixed. (Not a drink in the place, of course.)

Four years ago, I'd have been leading deputations.

When I arrived back in Ireland, I discovered something else – the pure joy of being able to talk and be understood. I remember stopping on a road at the foot of Mount Brandon in Kerry to talk to a man cutting bushes. I wanted to make sure my discovery was real. It was. And I talk to my own people at Sunday Mass in their own accent. My sisters are a bit ashamed of my brogue, and my mother is proud of me, although, being deaf, she can't hear a word I say, but she sees the people listening.

After a while I decided to stop living off the people of Brackile – my family and relatives – and left Mother and the thatched house for a week or so to meet a few friends who drink a beer or two and talk about anything but the quality of hay and the price of cattle. A middle-aged man I met recently at home – husband of the lady who runs the local tavern – almost blew up in my face as we were driving four miles to see a movie in Cappamore.

'Jesus,' says he, 'I'm listening to them talking about the scarcity of grass and the drop in pigs and the wetness of the weather for six nights of the week. I escape it sometimes by rushing into the parlour and belting shite out of the piano for two hours. But that's no good; a man has to get out.'

The movie was lousy but it did him good.

The deadness and lifelessness of winter brought on a kind of Teutonic gloom on me too, but since I joined my friends in the Navan area I've had some great, honest, lively sessions with people struggling in more colourful areas of life than mine. Last night I got a great kick out of hearing Frank McNamara, a priest of Meath diocese and a top-class organist (the only Fellow of the Royal College of Organists ever to play Gaelic football in Croke Park!) proclaim, 'What the hell difference does it make whether it's F Sharp or F Flat when the Gospel imperative is to feed the hungry, visit the sick, etc.'

Yesterday I went chasing off after biblical filmstrips (to take back to Philippines with me) and ended up on the wintry shore of a lake at midnight with a delightfully airy but unprofligate young nun. We talked and talked about our roles in the Church and it gave both of us great happiness.

The greatest kick I got, however, was last week, when I turned down a job I would have grabbed three years ago when I felt lost and irrelevant during my early stages in Subic – being editor of a monthly magazine for Irish diocesan priests called *Intercom*. Toeing party lines is not my bag, and working directly under the Irish bishops would be big-time toeing. Some sweaty night in two years' time, when my third successive project has failed in Santa Cruz and the tropical God is as far away and as cold as the polar ice cap, I'll probably kick myself for not accepting it. But what the hell! Life has to be lived now.

You know, Annette, I'm half-afraid to meet you – you are so like what I want to be. You talk about me being spontaneous, but there's a keenness and buoyancy and exuberance and gentleness floating through your letters which I envy. Yes, of course I've got into trouble. I make enemies, but I also make great friends. Not enemies in the sense that someone goes for one's spear but people who live in closed ranks get their hackles up if I lob a firecracker into their *esprit de corps*. You would do the same thing at a staff meeting, but I think you would be better able to bounce your way into a breezy reconciliation.

There were a lot of times since you began writing when I felt that not only would it be refreshing to meet you, but that I would find some sort of mirror-image of myself in you.

By the way, how did ye get the gold leaf on the Christmas card? Did ye airbrush it on or rub it on, having glued the protective figures first and then peel them off? A very professional job, anyway, and congratulations to the artists. That's what education is all about. It's a pity so many parents love their children by rushing off to the shops and spending money on finished products for them.

I have a niece, Patricia, aged six and a half, and she has got the greatest kick out of a claw hammer, a few pounds of one-and-a-half-inch nails and ends of planed wood from a building site. She doesn't have time to make all the things she thinks of. The last products I saw as I was leaving were STOP, GO and DETOUR signs, made and painted for some imaginary road.

Dalgan Park, 9 January 1975

I was out again last night, dispelling the winter gloom, with a small, mixed group: Christy and Mary Foley, J.W. and a contemporary of all of us, Rhona McManus, whose connection with us began as a partner in mixed-foursomes golf. Christy started life as a blacksmith and while he has now extended the business into wrought ironwork, he still holds on to the same brutal honesty one finds in good craftsmen.

Mary, his wife, has a fatal cancer in the vertebrae, and while she is having all sorts of punishing treatments,

131

she is miraculously the life and soul of any gathering. I had sat up into the early morning with Christy a few nights previously – talking mainly about Mary – and it came to me that I had never realised what true love between husband and wife was like until it was explained to me by this 'rough diamond'. Strangely enough, it gave me tremendous hope in my own vocation.

J.W. is a shy, prudent, intelligent fellow and we've been the best of friends for the past fifteen years, because he has always been a foil to my up-and-down temperament. I seem to do things in extremes. I cannot plod a steady path. If I paint a picture, I have to do it in fifteen minutes or fail. With me, things have to be done under inspiration or by intuition, never with cold logic. Like you, I respond to the thought of the grand gesture with exhilaration, but get into a lot of trouble over it. If I don't grab the moment now, it's always too stale to recreate it.

Last night all of us went out for a meal, and Rhona underestimated the strength of a third Manhattan, so I had to take her out of the restaurant and walk her up and down under the moonlight in Carrickmacross. It only made her worse. She saw a wrought-iron seat in front of somebody's house and headed for it. I sat holding her while she composed herself. It was great because it was real – even when the Garda came, carefully scrutinised us and then walked on.

As I reread these few pages, I realise how untypical it is for me, compared with my very humdrum life. I suspect, though, that life only gives us, at most, a few hours on the high wire, and the rest of the day is spent plodding the grass. But God help the man or woman who never experiences the heights, or, worse still, who spends most of the time up there.

I have no calendar at hand here, but I will be in London in the first week of March and I will stay with you. Seamus is meeting me on the first Friday in March. He's studying in the University of Swansea – something to do with economics and development in the Third World – and cannot get away until the weekend. I know you have class, but in spite of that, I may arrive with you between 2 and 4 March and housekeep for you while you earn our daily bread. If I write or telephone you, could you meet me at the airport, and should I get an afternoon or evening flight? I haven't got my visa re-approved yet.

I still have to dig into many things, not least of which are the Xerox copies of our appeal for the craft centre. You're a darling for trying. Right now a classmate of mine – and a roaring alcoholic – is here with me and I must steer him safely somewhere.

This letter is a regular mess, but I do guarantee to keep you up late some nights, in early March, in continuation. Greetings to Miguel, Purita, Inigo, a warm hello to Eileen and love and respect to you, my friend.

Jim

Brackile, Pallasgrean, County Limerick
25 February

Dear Annette,

You are as prolific as St Augustine in thought and word. It brightened me up to think that you would dash off fourteen pages for me, and with observations all over the place that

133

find an echo in me – 'I hate anything cold and calculated . . .' or ' . . . the knowledge that I've never run away' or 'When I'm unhappy I punish myself' (That's why I never drink when I'm sad!) or 'To put one's faith in one man (or woman) is fatal without an eternal or universal dimension' or 'I have a very cold streak in me too – everything for some, nothing for others' or 'But no one is ever going to make me believe that chastity is pleasing to God.'

I'll leave the rest for the pub. If things work out, I plan to reach London on Saturday 1 March and stay until the following Friday. Seamus Connolly is coming up from Swansea. I would like you to meet him because he has a rare mind and is far more decisive and honest than I. He comes the Thursday before I leave for Vietnam. I have no plans whatsoever for London, except to see you and the brood and Seamus.

I met your friend Magdalen, and not at the foot of the cross either. I went to Navan for a funeral and to do a rehash writing job for a group helping out in the drought-stricken Sahel region of West Africa, so I looked her up and took her to Christy and Mary Foley's. We left there at 2 AM.

Her convictions didn't scare me stiff, but Magdalen seems to have no loose ends hanging about. She seems to be the perfect modern nun theologically and emotionally – with the proper poise, the permitted flexibility. Her 'furniture' is like that of a modern kitchenette: clean-lined, chromium-plated and without a single threadbare settee in sight.

Christ Almighty, can one be that perfect and confident? Or is it that she is English? On second thoughts, maybe her convictions do scare me stiff too. However, she was a breath of fresh air, she dumbfounded Foley and said a lot of nice things about you. You'll laugh at this: I had pictured you at 5' 1" and plump. Magdalen put me straight. I had to call her Magdalen, too – none of this 'Patsy' stuff.

I wish I could go to Spain with ye and prowl around, unshaven. If the proposition had come up last August or September, I'd have begged and borrowed to do it, because it's the only country I want to walk through.

You'll have to soliloquise for me about loss of love and rejection, because I have never felt it. I have a foreboding that some day I will pay for having had a happy and unruffled life. I do believe that the commitment to marriage is far, far greater and more responsible than Magdalen's or mine. The biggest problem about love and marriage is to know how to work at them. Congratulations on getting, more or less, the house that you wanted. I think you are a decisive woman. God knows you need to be now.

I did fumble the ball a bit in my use of the '*tristis post coitum*' statement. A man's judgement about his love for a woman is truer the less sensual it is, and at no time is he less sensual than during the *TPC*. I may have seemed to be advocating pre-marriage sex and downgrading sensuality, but I don't mean it that way. It's just that a few marriage cases I came across recently highlighted the torture of partners discovering who they really were after six years of marriage. They didn't really know one another, and the equipment for knowing had gone rusty.

I'm anxiously awaiting my re-entry papers to the Philippines. I will telephone you when I have final arrangements made.

It's only during the last month at home that I've become conscious of the strain of leaving the old house and my mother and a square mile of land more familiar to me than anywhere else in the world.

In our family, our emotions are held tightly in check, but we feel deeply. There is nothing I wouldn't do for any of them, except admit to them that I love them. That must be some kind of psychological block, but since all of us follow that kind of pattern, we all know what we feel.

I notice you have reverted to your family surname, Rowland. I hope your cynicism about men being sods does not rule out forever the possibility that some time you may, once again, find a new one, and this time find the fullness of life.

Love, Jim

Moatlands, Navan (J.W.'s place)
20 February 1975

This has to be quick, and by the time it reaches you I will have telephoned you anyway. I finalised travel arrangements yesterday – a little different from what I anticipated. I arrive London on 6 March at 7.30 PM, timed so you would be finished school and have your chores done. I leave 11 March for Paris and Saigon.

You will receive a parcel in a few days, and don't be mad at me when you open it. I never buy anything, save books, cigarettes and wine, so don't hold this extravagance against me. You probably have the house cluttered with delft but since this set took my fancy, I hope you will like them. I am not a 'gifty' man but one does get the urge to give part of oneself to a close and kindred spirit.

I brush all your warnings out of the way. You're still Annette, who has been writing to me. 'Priests, generally speaking, only mix with rather prim and proper people, don't they?' Sweet Jesus, that took the wind out of me. Aye, I too am descended from a long line of prim and proper people! Wouldn't you know that from my letters?

I hope you will be at the airport. I'm a bit helpless at airports – not at all the James Bond type. Generally my clothes don't fit, people ignore me and I'm usually going in the wrong direction.

I'm on a last fling here.

Love, Jim

Six hours out of London
12 March 1975

Dear Annette,

It was just like you to wait on and give me that final wave of farewell. By now you will probably have collapsed from fatigue. I've had no transit problems and am quite resolved to stay a while in Vietnam, bleak and all as the situation looks there. I've found nothing to alter my view of French stewardesses; those on this journey with me are also arrogant and humourless. I'm not in a bad mood now. I was very sad leaving you. It's natural that one so warm and straight should have that effect on me. You are a proof of death and resurrection in life. You give people hope. I got it from you. So many of us are clingers and moaners. I don't idealise you. I'm just glad that our journeys criss-crossed and we paused a little at the crossing.

Tel Aviv

We're refuelling and can't leave the aircraft. I've an Indian businessman beside me. He stood me five beers before lunch and both of us would have been plastered had I let him continue.

'I love to drink. It frees me from care,' he said.

Looking at the countries stamped on his passport – from Zambia to Venezuela – it's no wonder he has cares. He's in the rag trade.

I met a group of Filipino dancers going from Amsterdam to Bombay. We are great friends now, because I spoke to them in Filipino. It's a bit sad, in a way, that they should appreciate – with shrieks of delight – a foreigner speaking their language. I wonder would I have shrieked if you had burst forth in Irish last night?

You did say one very touching thing: how nice it was to cuddle up on a sofa with someone you know you can trust. It was a great compliment to me – and a great pleasure, in case I forget.

I didn't ask you what you thought of me. I couldn't do that. One thing did emerge loud and clear: you could buy and sell me. Must be your Foreign Office training! I'll write now to my mother and Alice. Happy and safe trip back from Spain, and may God give food to the hungry.

Love, Jim

Dear Annette,

I'm at a loose end, waiting for the St Patrick's festivities to detonate, and while I have a lot of the normal correspondence before me to reply to, I'm not in the humour for it. How the hell are you?

At thirty-five thousand feet over the Bay of Bengal, I felt I was going in the wrong direction. The absurdity of me being relevant in the East – except in the most modern form of witch doctor – was clearly and devastatingly revealed to me in one of those flashes. In that mood, I felt like writing to 'Shameless' and saying, 'For — sake, stay back there with the Annettes, even if you do have to publish.'

Further on in the flight, the captain told us to look out the port windows and we saw Phnom Penh burning.

I move out to Zambales in a few days without fear or trembling. Reality has returned to me, flawed and all as it is. I did all my trembling in Saigon. Even though there are no signs of panic there, I sensed doom. Admiration always surges up in me for people who refuse to lie down and say, 'Pity us.' You are a case in point, but the Vietnamese I met brought it home more forcefully.

There was no teeth-gritting, only a silent, dignified adjustment to circumstances. An old man from Danang: 'I had five thousand mango trees. It pleased me to give fruit to my friends, to anyone. The Americans burned them all. Now, I buy fruit like everyone else.'

I dined over a low table in a hotel room with Thu Thuy Ngo, whom Seamus knows as Sister Theresia, the nurse. We had pigeon. She fed me with chopsticks and I saw nothing out of the ordinary when she deliberately chewed the pigeon's head, beak and all. 'This is a young pigeon,' she explained. 'The bones are soft and can be chewed.'

We clung to one another in Manila in 1971 for a month or two. She nursed me when I was sick after a painful operation, and from a do-or-die language course. She felt isolated too. She disliked the Filipinos, and her Vietnamese pride took a lot of stick in the convent where she was quartered. Through her I got a great insight into the Eastern woman.

You think you frighten men? Well let me tell you that you are a cuddly teddy bear compared to this 4' 7" meek Vietnamese virgin. This time we behaved very properly. She only left a beautiful set of teeth marks on my upper lip. They turned black and I still have them. She laughed graciously and said I was like Padre Pio with the stigmata.

'He is dead, you know,' she added.

'I never heard it,' says I.

Intrigue! Her capabilities there would make the CIA blush. She managed to stay with me, stay with her mother and stay in a convent all at the one time. The end is nigh and I think she wanted to whoop it up. She conned the hotel into giving me free lodging, but I drew the line at free board. She bought ten pairs of shoes for my nieces and a black elephant-skin handbag for Alice for half-nothing, and airmailed them to Ireland. She walked behind me in public places but imperiously gave orders to me behind closed doors. She painlessly denuded my suitcase of many odds and ends while she meticulously repacked.

When she smiled at something, I nodded and it was put to one side. Her mother sent baskets of fruits and two marble elephants from the mountains of Danang. I left her with a mixture of sadness and relief. She was something beautiful and strange and an unsophisticate like me needed to experience her likes to open my eyes a little wider. After you and Thu, both my eyes are as wide as full moons now.

I talked with her for two hours through the Customs grille at the airport – like a visitor at a Carmelite monastery. I had to blow my nose when the call came to board. She just smiled goodbye and I know I shall never see her again.

One thing, though – when the Communists do come she will slide through their catechism and con them too. Good luck to her and God bless her.

12.30 AM

The suicide impulse wasn't very strong in me tonight. I went to a low-key but very enjoyable party at a popular port of call for Columbans, None and Noreen Trota's place. Noreen is a Kerrywoman and None is a Filipino. I came home early – before the Irish contingent began to sing.

Now that I've had my few celebratory Scotches, I'd like to return to something I wanted to explain to you before I left. Like myself, you too get the impulse to destroy yourself because you are the antithesis to a humdrum girl. The affair after that gutless priest's running away was a case in point. You have lived in the apogee of failure and rejection, but you do have a character and spirit that is wonderful. Annette, I'm not pie-eyed or making a romantic pitch. I have enough on my hands with Alice, who has

141

never been buffeted by raw, brutal life. You do have a nobility in you which you must always trust intuitively. You are a big and beautiful woman, and it crucified me to think that you do not have a man yet who is the equal of you. I will pray that you find him, not a bloody priest. Most are oddballs, needing mothers more than wives.

I wrote to you twice about Alice. That, I needed to reveal to someone, a sympathetic confessor. Your affirmation of her, in thought and in deed, was important to me. I had lived so much in secret. I hate furtiveness. I love loyalty and would, I hope, stand by it even though it shattered me.

I thank you for giving me your mind, your time, your home. I loved the last night – our lives are so barren. I will mooch around Spain with you some time and take whatever the consequences are because, like Alice, you have affected me and I can't brush it away with prayer and hair shirts. I am illogical and a fool and I think now I'm a bit pissed.

I will write to you when I am settled in Zambales. Don't know yet where it will be.

Jim

11

St Michael's Church, Santa Cruz, Zambales
8 April 1975

Dear Annette,

I've been holding myself back from answering your Valencia letter of 23 March principally because I've been expecting a permanent appointment and therefore a stable address.

Yesterday it came to pass, so for the next four years, my home will be a small town called Candelaria, five miles south of here in the mango-tree belt. It's a one-man parish, well fitted out by my predecessor, a seventy-plus old China hand who has a penchant for concrete and paint, my greatest weaknesses. It looks a nice place and I'll tell you about it later on. In accepting it – because I could have stayed in Santa Cruz – I deliberately picked the short straw. More about that, too, when I unravel my motives.

In spite of 95 degrees of heat and the post-vacation blues – it does take a few months to readjust – I seem to have stumbled out of no man's land now and have a foot on the straight and narrow until 1979.

It meant a lot to me that you could grab an interlude to write, because I know that you are having anything but a vacation. Why should you be worried by the impression I give of idealising you? I do think you are one of the liveliest

143

and most conscientious people I have ever met. I'll say this now and I'll never mention it again: celibacy for me has always been a permanent commitment on a tentative basis, meaning that if, at any stage of my life, I met a woman bigger than myself, one for whom my respect was so high that she could lead or drive me and liberate the hibernating horsepower I know is in me, it would be sinful not to team up with her in marriage – conventional or unconventional.

Male chauvinism, you may say, but it's the truth. In any deep friendship I've ever had with a woman, I've always been the partner prodding and goading the other to produce. It's like that with Alice. She doesn't push me and I need pushing. I need her to say to me, write a book, a play, paint a picture, and to keep prodding until I do.

It has been a great deprivation in my life to have no one to push me, because I am lazy. I often excuse myself by saying, what good is it staying up there all the time on a high? My family are the same. We seem to opt for the hard slog because it's simpler.

At forty-plus I've thrown in the towel on the really creative area and am content with the conventional products. That's why Alice and myself can keep going. She has developed by being prodded by my affection. It is good for her, but I'm sinking into a morass, production-wise.

But you frightened me, and I would not want to live close to you for long right now, because, right or wrong, I do see in you a woman of power for what you could make me do if you got out the whip. (I'm not thinking of de Sade's whip, actually.) I've lived a sheltered life, away from intellectual stimulation by a woman, which, based on all you've said and written and how you've ruled your life, you seem well able to do. Perhaps I'm only making excuses for my own inertia, and perhaps, too, if I did get the chance I'd lie down like a mule and wouldn't get up.

I told you about Alice because what has been plunging around one's heart and mind needs to be clarified in the light of day. I'm no nearer a solution, but the confession was therapeutic. The only commitment I have, I suppose, is like yours: to work our asses off and to give as complete a love as we can to humanity, with a special loyalty and intimate extras to the special people in our lives.

You described me as a somewhat old-fashioned (romantic) idealist. Shhh! Between ourselves, I'm a wolf in sheep's clothing waiting to get you behind the bushes. I'm not the only one you see with a monopoly on idealising! Let's have a competition and prove how black-hearted, masochistic, deceitful, lustful, greedy, etc. we really are. You first!

You are dead right when you say our circle should widen, but it's so difficult to find freed-up friendship or love. Your sister is a shrewd hussy to make that pragmatic remark about '79. By God, I won't let you off the hook either, and walk Spain we will. I want to live for a week, at least, before I die. Do you think I could borrow a broken-winded horse and a timber lance?

Annette, God bless you. Share my affection with your children. A special enquiry for Roger and S. That girl is beautiful, a welcoming, innocent angel separated from the pack.

Do angels travel in packs, anyway?

Best wishes,

Jim

St Michael's Church, Santa Cruz, Zambales
25 April 1975

Dear Annette,

I sat down here at the kitchen table to ponder, pencil at hand, how I will explain *I am the way, the truth and the life* to the people of Santa Cruz next weekend. I got distracted. The first blessed rains of the season stole in over the mountains on my blind side and literally cascaded down. Their cleansing, cooling feeling gave me great happiness. The first rain is considered medicinal, at least by the children, who romped naked in it.

Imagine being in the Sahel region of West Africa, with cattle dying and children getting skinnier, and waiting eight years for rain like this.

A US Navy jet screamed over, flying low to or from some carrier in the short span of water between here and Vietnam. The evacuation must be beginning. I had one letter – probably the last – from Thu Thuy. It was so sad. Herself and the mother never got back to Danang. Her father, sister and brother are there. I saw a letter from another St Paul de Chartres nun in Vietnam. It was a terrified appeal to get some of the congregation out. In some town, the name of which I can't remember, the Vietcong shot priests, brothers and sisters on taking power.

Five years ago I was a bit pink. The *convento* in Subic was a meeting place for armchair Maoist (Filipino version) revolutionaries and active ones during '71 and '72. Never again. They tried to use me. And then I read Solzhenitsyn's *Cancer Ward* and met my all-time hero of fiction, Kostoglotov, a man who insisted on the freedom of his mind, the freedom to write a poem and have it read. I'll go back to the way, the truth and the life again.

28 April

I got up this morning and your missing letter was on the kitchen table – someone coming from Manila must have dropped it off.

In the end, I felt I couldn't explain the way, the truth and the life, so I spoke on repentance as being a prerequisite for friendship with God. Not grovelling repentance, more an honest self-appraisal, and through it one takes the first step towards accepting Christ as the way, the truth and the life. I took the angle of repentance being a privilege, an achievement for the big-hearted, not for the weak-kneed. In view of what I said about the Communists, it was a coincidence that you contributed your tuppence-worth in today's letter. Aye, a few years under the Communists would be a very good thing. But how can you order a few years, and what about people like Thu Thuy who will be minced, the same as the corrupt rich? That's the dilemma.

Business: I've been checking up on my scholarship fund and the following payments are recorded from you since I went to Ireland. I acknowledge them with a kiss and a hug.

28/8/1974	£15
31/10/1974	£10
31/12/1974	£10
21/2/1975	£10

Rosella was with me for a day recently. Her total college expenses for last year were £160, a summary of which she submitted to me, complete with receipts. Her fund is lined up for next year, during which she will concentrate on agriculture and ceramics. She has two years to go.

I'm now going to make a specific request to the people in Hull, having surveyed the new scene here:

1. Training of another boy in basket-weaving and wood-polishing.
2. Establishment of a craft centre in Candelaria to specialise in one high-class product for export – probably a combination of weave and black hardwood with inlay. It will take a year, at least, before we have experimented enough to provide samples. I'll get cracking on it as soon as I move down to Candelaria. The address there is St Vincent's Church.

I'll be on my own there. It has its advantages, but I do like having somebody to fight with. Seamus and myself were at war regularly, but then we'd talk ourselves out of it. Some day I'll try to explain the isolation and psychological traumas that befall a foreigner here. I also want to tease out this idea of yours: that by going abroad to a Third World country, chasing an ideal, one somehow finds a more fulfilling and more perfect way of life.

I don't believe that. Surbiton is a bigger challenge than Candelaria. You'd be surprised at the number of people who, by fleeing the stress and complexities of modern

European society, are actually escaping to the Candelarias of the Third World just for a simple life. Maybe a simple life is a more perfect way of life.

I talked recently to Josefa Aldana, a great young nun I worked with in Subic, about a commune I'd like to form of my own chosen people in a valley out here. You and Seamus and she would be included among a group of seven men and seven women. It was damned attractive, but I concluded we'd be too volatile for it to survive more than a year. And what would we be doing anyway but helping ourselves?

Since I arrived in Santa Cruz, there has been an average of three to four children's funerals a week out of a population of thirty thousand. Dysentery and broncho-pneumonia are the main killers. That's where the action is. We run a barefoot-doctor service for TB victims, another killer. We show movies on child health, and although two no-nonsense young nuns work themselves to the bone in the barrios, the death rate is still savage. Birth control, even if promoted by the churches, is unacceptable. I promote responsible parenthood, and I've a stack of contraceptive products available so that the senior boys and girls in the school are aware of their existence.

The problem is the culture of the extended family as a solution for economic problems. I get the impression Filipinos don't think of tomorrow, and if you don't have that as motivation to change, it's hard to know where to start.

Love to Purita, Miguel and Inigo. Did you get your hands on *The Drifters?* Haven't read a decent book in months.

Love, Jim

12

It is only since 1975 that I have seen John Curry for the man he is. When I joined him in Santa Cruz, after returning for my second term in Philippines, I didn't know him that well. He had been the Columban superior while I was in Subic, a hard-working and decent fellow, but one I didn't always agree with. Dick Cannon, an American, had just replaced him in the job.

I had never felt completely at ease with superiors. All this secrecy and council meetings in order to reach conclusions was exclusive, and turned me off. I was for an up-front leadership, more consensus and more transparency. The Church, I felt, had to get out of the habit of governing from behind closed doors, and had to stop treating grown men and women like children if it was to retain credibility with the new generation.

It was interesting, therefore, to see the pastor rather than the superior side of John in this huge, active parish of many facets, which had enough work for three or four men. He had a great record as a caring, committed pastor. He had a full and clear agenda, and drove himself very hard.

I remember being at a fiesta with him on one of the islands off Santa Cruz. We had gone out there by *banca*. While I surveyed the scene and strolled around the small island to get my bearings, John was already focussed on the job and was organising the sequence of events to follow. I asked myself, 'Does this guy ever let up?'

Then, seeing me with my hands in my pockets he said, 'Would you like to hear a few Confessions?'

There was scarcely room on the island for sin.

The difference between John and me was that he had been more than twenty years in Zambales and he knew where his agenda started and where it finished. Even though there was only ten years between us in age, Vatican II had come between us. I had spent much of my time in Subic wondering whether I was on the right track theologically, whether I was part of the problem or part of the solution. John had no such doubts. Apart from responding to the main sacramental needs of people, and to ad hoc emergencies, I had no agenda I could call my own. Like Seamus, I believed a lot of the stuff we were doing was magic, and I wanted time to think about it.

With Curry, you didn't get time to think.

Holy Week came and we were incredibly busy. He did more than half the parish work and was a hands-on director of the big parish high school, St Michael's.

With only the Easter Sunday ceremonies to go, I saw him flop down on a chair in the *sala* on Saturday night, utterly whacked. He had the runs again, and his ulcer was acting up. I could see the remains of the white powder antacid on his lips. We decided I would be the one to get up at 4 AM for the big event of Easter Sunday, the *Salubong*.

The *Salubong* goes back to the 'liturgical theatre' devised by the Spanish friars to hammer home Christian truths such as the Resurrection. At 4 AM, before dawn, the Risen Christ would be carried in procession around one side of the town and back to the church. At the same time, another procession with Our Lady, outfitted in black veil as a sign of mourning, would leave the opposite end of the big church plaza, travel through another part of the town and back to the church. Then, with timing only the parishioners could accomplish after four hundred years' experience, Mother would meet Son in triumph.

John explained what I was to look out for in the dark.

Both statues and their carriages would be brought, all decorated by their owners, to opposite ends of the plaza for the start, and I was to walk with one of the processions – I can't remember now which one. John had explained to me in no uncertain terms why.

The owners of one of the statues and its carriage were currently at odds with him. They had set up a *nipa* nightclub on the edge of town, which was allegedly offering the services of a whorehouse. John had talked to them without effect, but they owned the statue and carriage and it would cripple the dawn drama if he banned them. So he warned me, 'On no account must you give them credibility by joining them.'

I said OK and went to bed.

It was really dark when I got down to the plaza at 4 AM. People holding lighted candles were milling around, and suddenly I couldn't remember which statues I should and shouldn't travel with. I didn't dare go back upstairs and wake up John, so I thought of a plan. If this crowd were club-owners and whorehouse merchants, they should look like sleazeballs. I'd seen enough of them in Subic.

I inspected both teams of men who were lining up to pull the carriages, and sure enough there they were, with well-trimmed little moustachios, hair slicked back with brilliantine and Teddy-boy outfits. With a slight shiver I joined the other team and everything went off like clockwork.

In an hour we were back at the main plaza. The statue of the Sorrowful Mother passed under a decorated bamboo archway and stopped. A little girl dressed as an angel was then lowered in harness from a secret niche in the arch. She removed the black veil of Mary to reveal a white one underneath. The joyous meeting (*salubong* in Filipino) between Mother and Son then took place to a chorus of Hosannas from the children's choir. Dawn was just breaking.

I said the first Mass at 6 AM and as I was going upstairs for breakfast, feeling happy with myself, John was coming down. He didn't wish me Happy Easter but bored me with his eyes and said, 'Why did you walk with that shower of hoors?'

I'd made the wrong choice and the stairs was the worst place in the world to look for a hole to bury myself in.

I hadn't yet adjusted to the Filipino breakfast, which was coffee and *pan de sal*, or rice and fish. A supermarket in Olongapo sold rashers and I had lost so much of myself in adapting to Philippines that I was determined to hold on to the rasher-and-egg part for as long as possible.

I was on my second rasher when Kieran Heneghan came in from Olongapo, because I had asked him to brief me about Santa Cruz, where he had been parish priest for eight years and had built the high school. Pedro, the cook, began fixing him breakfast enthusiastically, as they were old friends. Columbans always felt free to stop off at any parish for a meal or a drink, and this had one positive result: no matter how you felt about food or drink yourself, you always had to have something in stock for the visitors.

We covered a lot of ground, leaving a customary vagueness. Old hands never insisted that new guys should follow their footsteps exactly.

'Problems?' I asked.

He had his own problems, one time, he said, but they might not be mine. Guisguis was a big farming barrio, nine miles north-east of Santa Cruz town centre. It had its own church in the heart of rice-and-vegetable country, and was reached through bad roads and mud paths. Kieran had been edging his barrio congregation, mostly women, along the road towards *aggiornamento* on the last Sunday of every month, when he used to say Mass there. The idea was to detach them a little from San Guillermo, their barrio patron, to whom they gave total support, and lead them towards Christ in the Mass and the Eucharist. He had a packed house the Sunday he began his campaign. The old women nodded their heads and murmured approval, as he went on to extol Christ-centred devotions over *santo*-centred devotions.

When he had finished and began the offertory, the same old women who had nodded their approval so supportively got up from their pews and, as usual, went to the statue of San Guillermo, lit him his candles and started to say the rosary in front of him. Before the Consecration, the minibus that carried the women who sold the vegetables in town pulled in, and another third of the congregation left in a hurry, picked up their vegetables outside the door and piled in. Kieran was left with one third of his attendance for the Christ-centered devotion of the Mass. He looked down and knew his message had missed the target, and would keep missing the target until he could deal with San Guillermo himself. He was getting so frustrated, the thought occurred to him that he might remove the statue altogether.

An opportunity came later in the month, when he went back to Guisguis to survey typhoon damage. The big doors of the church were banging in the wind. An old lady was kneeling before the statue of San Guillermo, her candles flickering desperately in the struggle to stay alive.

She continued to pray for some time, then quenched her candles and saw him. She kissed his hand in respect. He spoke to her, with the respect words added in Ilocano, her dialect. He told her what the Pope and cardinals were doing in Rome and, in particular, what they were saying about the *santos* of the Church.

'What are they saying, Father?'

'That they can be a distraction and are hogging the limelight from Christ.'

'Even our San Guillermo, Father?'

Kieran, cute Mayoman, paused before replying – with another question. 'What would you say if I took him away with me?'

She didn't bat an eyelid. 'I have a small one at home which will do in the meantime.'

'What do you mean by "in the meantime"?' Kieran persisted.

'It was your predecessor who gave us this statue, Father. Your successor will surely return him to us.'

'You'll have to decide now, Jim, whether San Guillermo is bigger than Jesus or not!' Kieran said with a twinkle in his eye.

The Columbans weren't friars; they were journeymen, coming and going, and were no match at all for old women with long memories.

Kieran is now retired in Ireland and has remained, of all our Columban friends, the best. He shares, with my wife, a faith I cannot yet reach, but enjoys the multitude of views we have in common.

The graph of the Columban Society's membership, rising to over a thousand since 1918, curved and turned backwards during my Philippine years. It was sudden and it was irreversible.

The Church, complacent and cumbersome, sat it out, and to this day has not made an objective and public analysis of the causes of the exodus. Neither has the Society. The reason I can say that with conviction is that none of us who left have ever been asked about it. During all the Society chapters and conventions since the mid-seventies, planning for the future, no paper pinpointing causes has emerged. None of us has ever been consulted and it cannot be done without us. Between 1969 and 1977, 170 priests left the Society and the priesthood. No one, to my knowledge, traced the reasons for this to their logical sources. Can anyone imagine corporate business closing its eyes to a personnel haemorrhage like that?

When I arrived in Candelaria in 1975, I wasn't aware of the scale of what was happening. There were no notices pages anywhere to provide information, because a priest leaving the Society, for whatever reason, was all hush-hush. It was treated like a disease which might only alarm people if they knew. The prevailing attitude among the priests in the know – superiors and their councils – was that it might be embarrassing for the people concerned to have the information released. There was no thought for the devastating conclusions people might come to in ignorance – that the guy was a paedophile, that he had raped some girl, or robbed the church building fund.

Some guys left softly-softly, inch-by-inch.

They took a leave of absence – to think things over, to study, to get a feel of real life – but ultimately, few came back. It was a sensible way to do it. It gave time for them and their families to adjust to psychological and economic realities.

As I settled in in Candelaria, a lot more was happening

that I didn't know about, or had only vaguely heard of. Three more young Australians – Mick Schell, who worked in the Manila area, and Chris Papworth and Neil Frazer who worked in Mindanao – were on their way out. Schell, who was as handsome as Gregory Peck and had flocks of *dalagas* in his way every time he was out and about, married an Australian girl in Australia. Neil stayed on in Mindanao and married a Filipina. Peter Fitzpatrick, a young American, married another Filipina and stayed on in Manila as a personnel consultant to a banking group. Hynes and Healy, who worked in Negros and Mindanao respectively, peeled away from official parish duties to work for 'the Movement', as they called it. The Movement was a Marxist–Maoist-style revolution in the building, until it fizzled out prematurely after the fall of the Berlin Wall. Then the plain people of Manila, hijacking the revolt idea, ousted Marcos peacefully and installed Cory Aquino after the famous 'People Power' stand-off of 1988. Both Hynes and Healy married Filipinas and eventually returned to Ireland.

Some of my best friends, now living in the Dublin area, were preparing to break the link too around that time. Joe O'Grady, who had worked in Pangasinan, was in London, considering his future, still a priest. Tony O'Dwyer was also in London, preparing to take the plunge. He had been in Castillejos, next door to Subic, while I was there. Both left later and married. Hilary Shannon, Donal MacDonald, Barry O'Hagan and John O'Connell, who were still in Philippines, would soon be ready for take-off too. Little did I know then that I would soon be among them.

St Vincent's Parish, Candelaria, seemed an easy number, but would not have the buzz of Subic, especially a Subic with

Seamus around. It would have a bigger land area to be covered, but only half the people to look after. It had been part of Masinloc parish to the south at one time, and many Zambalenos still thought of it only as a big barrio. The streets were laid out in blocks, American style. Some were paved, some were earthen and a few had only grass The church was new, built by my classmate, Paddy O'Herlihy, in the sixties. The timber-frame high school was in good shape, and the *convento*, added to by Con, was adequate. What more could a man ask for?

I took my time. Doc's advice about slowing down was beginning to work. The St Paul Sisters, who had a big reputation in Philippine education, ran the high school, St Vincent's Academy. I talked to Sister Gabriel, the principal, and she seemed happy when I suggested I would only get involved when she needed me – that the parish was my real job. One of her Sisters, Sister Carolyn, was in charge of the two parish catechists. All three of them covered religious education in the municipality's six elementary schools. Soling was first among equals among the women of the parish, a middle-aged unmarried lady who also ran the school canteen. I could really sit back if I wanted to. I talked to people, visited the barrios and essentially continued Con's routine until I was convinced otherwise.

That didn't take long. The long and the short of it was, I got bored. Bored with being a kind of a squire in a small, sleepy village. It was time I got dug in and made work for myself.

I consulted Kieran Heneghan, who had eight years' experience in Santa Cruz, about options. He had a flair for the social-action side of the ministry. He had started a TB-eradication scheme two years previously with drugs supplied by the Philippine Department of Health. If I had two 'barefoot doctors' trained, and could pay them, there was no reason why I couldn't begin, he told me. Kevin Farrissey, in Masinloc, was running the scheme successfully.

It was amazing how much the likes of Soling knew about the prevalence of TB in the municipality, even though – as in Ireland in the Noel Browne era – it was kept hidden.

We sent out information about the forthcoming sputum-testing through the mayor and barrio school principals. Two girls were trained as 'barefoot doctors' and I wrote to five friends in Ireland, one of whom was J.W., for £200 each to pay the salaries for a year. Four responded enthusiastically and immediately. It was the first time I ever put the squeeze on anyone, but I was stuck. The fifth, a high-ranking cleric in east Limerick, not only didn't respond, but complained to my mother about my cheek. In no time at all we were up and running without him.

While in Santa Cruz, Kieran had been running barrio movie shows at night on religious themes. The projector was powered by car batteries. The shows entertained and edified, but lacked one vital ingredient – feedback from the audience. Without feedback, I wouldn't proceed. After five years in Philippines, I knew it was vital. Religion was an intellectual as well as an emotional experience. It had to be offered as something which could be accepted or rejected, and that meant that there should be dialogue about it. I set about planning for it, and that's another story.

13

Candelaria, 18 October 1975

Dear Annette,

I read an article about Spain by Alistair Reid in the *New Yorker* and it's making me think of you and our plans for '79. It's time I wrote to you anyway.

I feel a bit blank these days. Seem to be without verve or colour. One should only feel like that when tiredness takes over. I go dead sometimes, even though I'm fit as a fiddle. I've been talking a lot lately among groups of priests and a sprinkling of nuns about the future of the missions and our role in them.

I find them to the left and right of me. A young fellow called me a liberal and made it sound like a bad word. In my work, I'm often nearer the evangelical right of the Baptists than the horizontal left of the World Council of Churches. If a priest is anything, he should be a prophet, like Amos or our Society's patron Columbanus. I'm considered left of centre because I question things. It's easy for me to do that. I have no precedents to follow, like the more seasoned missionaries.

Before I left here last Monday morning to attend the bishop's monthly meeting with his priests, I read in the *Manila Bulletin* that a little monthly magazine called the *Communicator* was closed down by Marcos. Edited by an

American Jesuit called Jim Reuter, it never took on an anti-Marcos crusading role. Without commentary, it just published damning facts.

When I got to the meeting, all the talk was about a proposed visit of Cardinal Sin to the town of Iba. The discussion about arrangements went on and on, and when it got to the colour of the vestments we were going to wear, I blew up. I said, 'Don't ye know that the last free media voice in the Philippines was suppressed last night and here we are discussing the colour of vestments!'

I proposed that we address ourselves to composing a letter of protest to Juan Ponce Enrile, the Philippine defence minister. We agreed that the bishop would write it and we'd approve it. He really surprised me by writing a great letter, adroit but trenchant.

After the meeting, I was offered the post of Director of Columban College in Olongapo, but turned it down, because I'm not a school person, not even administration material. I can't even manage myself. I've reached the limit of my ability here in Candelaria as *monsieur le curé* of eight thousand people.

I was in Manila last week (five and a half hours' drive) for the foundation of OCIC in the country. OCIC (*Office Catholique International du Cinema*) sponsors education and evangelisation through celluloid. I was really groping around for clues on how best to communicate to people who are nominally Catholic, but not churchgoers.

Maybe 'interact' is a better word than 'communicate'. I can communicate with you because there is a meeting of minds, and what you have to say to me is as important as what I have to say to you. I'm not trying to persuade you and I do not, therefore, modify my words to influence you. My communication with the barrio people has to be somewhat the same, otherwise it's manipulation.

I don't possess any panacea motivating me to manipulate people to my side for their good. I don't even know what's good for them. All I want to do is present a picture of their own lives to them, as an outsider, and let them reflect on it and come to conclusions about it – their conclusions, not mine.

It's the apathy, the fatalism here which has to be cracked. Religion practised within a social framework which is apathetic and fatalistic is, as Marx said, the opium of the people. Candelaria is apathetic because most of the people are locked into feudal land and social structures, which they cannot break out of. They are tenant farmers with no hope of owning the land or increasing their holdings. They are locked into family and interfamily loyalties, which take precedence over personal ambition.

Two of the Church's sacraments consolidate that – baptism and marriage. In both, the sponsors play a social role I've never come across in Ireland. The sponsors at baptism and marriage offer patronage; the child and the newly-weds take on obligations which are almost feudal. This means that lives are regulated from the top down, not from the bottom up.

The NPA (New People's Army) are exploiting this class structure. The suspicion I have about them is that they too will use the feudal mentality to keep power once they get it. I hope they don't ever hold power.

I had an experience recently here in Candelaria, and the staggering effrontery of it pissed me off, particularly because it was orchestrated by a fellow Columban, who shall remain nameless. He has close ties with the NPA. I admire him because of his courage and convictions. He has made a pro-Maoist revolution choice, like some other priests and nuns I know of, and he's sticking with it. Anyway, he left a Filipino friend of his with me for a few days, giving me some vague story that he was a Methodist and needed shelter for a while. In the missions, hospitality is given without question.

My visitor was scarcely gone when I discovered he was Jose Maria Sison, the founder of the new Communist Party of the Philippines, the author of a couple of books on the struggle against imperialism – a lot of their contents virulent anti-American doggerel. He wrote them under the appropriate name 'Amando Guerrero'. He has been underground since 1972, is currently Public Enemy Number One in the country and has a price on his head.

The point I'm slow in making is that the Marxist analysis of society as preached by the NPA is just another form of manipulation with an objective of power – and I was manipulated to save Sison's skin on the run. Bugger that! I therefore ask myself am I manipulating people in my apostolate here? It frightens me to think that I might be.

That is why I want to get down to the very roots, to slide projection and discussion, and try to get people to free themselves, to reach their own conclusions. The bright boys in the Church call this pre-evangelisation. I know people can't reach their own conclusions about everything. One or two would do me fine for a start – even if they make me redundant.

Anyway, I'm training Sister Carolyn (the head of catechetics and my *mulier fortis* in the evangelising business) as a photographer. Our slides are already making people sit up in the church. Carolyn is the anticipating-est woman I've ever worked with, and has saved me from ruin a couple of times. I was going off to explore a piece of the Zambales Mountains early one morning recently and she dragged me back, because it was the feast of the Assumption, a holy day of obligation. I had forgotten all about it. It's the first time I've had a working rapport with a woman and have been unaffected by her charm. She's so damn serious, there's no room left for charm!

I regretted afterwards that she intercepted me. The feasts of the Assumption and the Immaculate Conception in the church calendar should be treated like the month of February in the yearly calendar. They shouldn't be there.

Apart from this attempt at pre-evangelisation, I'm not sure where the challenge lies for me.

The most enterprising of Candelaria's barrios is Huacon, a farming and fishing community three miles to the north. Their language there is Ilocano, and when they speak it, I do not know what they're saying. They're generally quite good at English and would wish me to speak in English rather than in Filipino. The people around Candelaria town speak Zambal, a language I don't understand either. While in Subic, I knew what people were saying, but here I haven't a clue.

At Mass a few Sundays ago, my sermon was about the seed going into the ground and dying before it can spring up. The word for seed in Tagalog is '*buto*', with the same emphasis on either vowel. I mispronounced it, putting an emphasis on the 'u', which made it the Tagalog word for bone, a euphemism in the local languages for an erect penis. The congregation got a great laugh at the thought of an erect penis springing up out of the ground.

I say Mass in Huacon every Sunday evening at five, one hour before sunset and darkness. It has a big barn of a church, which is nearly always full. The participation and singing is good. There is only one problem: the congregation is made up of women and children. During the Mass, I look out the big wide doors and see the farmers riding home from the fields on their carabaos. They don't even look in, not to mention bless themselves. If I were at home in Brackile, I would be one of them. Here, I am irrelevant to them, and that makes me sad, because I am really one of them in spirit. One thing is sure: I'm not going to reach them through ritual and sacraments and Mass, the programme of Con.

While I'm telling you about my hectic life in Candelaria, I have to include another element of its make-up – superstition, which tested my mettle a month ago.

I was having a beer in the *sala* one evening with a group of elementary teachers who often come to visit me. Carolyn came up the stairs and told me there was a girl possessed by an evil spirit up the street, and would I go and bless her and say prayers over her. It was, she thought, one of our high-school students.

I could only gape in astonishment, 'That went out in the time of Jesus.' I didn't believe in evil spirits and wouldn't know how to confront one if I did.

'Father O'Connell would go,' she insisted.

'This must be some kind of hoax, Carolyn. Would

you ask Sister Gabriel to check it out and let me know what's behind it. It's school business.'

In half an hour, Gabriel was back. 'I'm afraid you'll have to come, Father. It is one of our students. She's in some kind of trance and is raving. There's a big crowd surrounding the house. People are saying she picked up the spirit of a man who died recently in the same street.'

Carolyn, ever efficient, came towards me with my white soutane, stole, holy water and the ritual. It was a wonder she hadn't it open at 'EVIL SPIRITS, THE EXORCISM OF'. I told Carolyn we'd have a look at this first without the religious paraphernalia, and then, maybe, if it developed into a serious confrontation between good and evil, I'd take advantage of my priestly armour-plating.

I walked down the wide street followed by the teachers and the nuns. As I passed each house, stragglers began to come out and follow. I turned right into the grass street where the girl lived. More people began swelling the group of teachers and nuns behind me, because the news had spread like wildfire. None of them would walk with me. I was in the lead by myself. I wasn't afraid, I just didn't know what I was going to do.

All I could think of was Clint Eastwood walking down the main street of some western town to have a shoot-out with the big *bandido*. The whole scene was ridiculous. I could feel the tension in the people. A normally noisy street had gone silent. When I got to the house, it was surrounded by people, six deep.

'Clear the stairs,' I muttered to Gabriel, who, being school principal, had far more authority in the town than I.

Most Filipino families in the barrios live on the first

166

floor. The downstairs is open, and used for storing agricultural stuff.

'I want everyone out of the house,' I said to no one in particular as I jostled my way up the wooden steps. That seemed a safe thing to say.

We went up and in. People were milling around. The place was hot. When Gabriel finally cleared everyone down to ground level, I saw a young girl, about sixteen, sitting on a form between her parents, who had their hands around her shoulders. She had a lighted candle in her hand and had some herbs or leaves stuffed down the front of her school uniform. I motioned to the parents to leave her to me.

I sat down beside her and put my arm around her. She was really in some kind of trance. The candle had melted a little, so that wax was seeping through her fingers. I took it away from her and began to talk to her in a fatherly and reassuring way in Filipino. For five minutes, I got no response, but I kept at it: 'Don't be afraid. You're going to be OK. Don't believe all this rubbish about evil spirits. You are a very good girl and no one would ever harm you. Don't even worry about the exams. I'll help so that you get good marks.'

Then an eye flickered, the first response. 'I have you now,' I said to myself, 'and whatever on earth was wrong with you is over now.'

She came to, still a bit dazed. I told her to call to see me in the morning before class and advised the parents to put her to bed. It was pitch dark anyway.

Next morning, a young lady I scarcely recognised breezed in and said, 'Father, you told me to call to see you

167

before I go to class. Here I am!' One would never think it was the same girl who brought the town to a standstill the night before.

I wondered would Con have got the same result in surplice, stole and holy water. He probably would.

See my problem, Annette? I think part of my job here is to get rid of religion.

How are your strays? Did you break any of our plates yet? Or go to sleep in the bath? Haven't heard from Alice in a while. She's collecting filmstrips for me. Do you know anywhere I could lay hands on educational strips on science – chemistry, physics, biology – and I wouldn't have to pay for them? I have equipped myself with a portable daylight screen and a projector powered by car battery. I scrounge for strips on pig rearing, nutrition, family planning, etc.

Rosella was here yesterday and we discussed the future of our crafts business. She is enthusiastic and will go to summer school for extra classes. She still doesn't believe in God.

I watched a vasectomy being done last week in Candelaria Rural Hospital, which I visit regularly. The doctor who was being shown how to do it for the first time had thick fingers and couldn't find the vein in question. It was a pantomime. I asked him why the scrotum of the about-to-be-vasectomised patient was purple. For some strange reason, it flashed across my mind that Filipinos might have purple balls.

'Mercurochrome, Father,' he said.

I felt an awful ass. I had a bad psychological reaction to the operation – as if the op was far more serious than met the eye.

On that seedy note, I leave you. Pardon the script.
I'm writing in bed again.

Love, Jim

Candelaria, 13 September 1975

Dear Annette,

Tomorrow, Sunday, I drive to Manila for the annual retreat,
and while there I'll continue this. Your recent typed letter
is so easy to read and you do get more into less space, so
keep it up. I find if I don't get down straightaway while
your words are hot in my mind, my reply, if delayed, will
focus on the preoccupations of the moment.

For instance, I wrote a shortie this afternoon to my
friend J.W. (Mary Foley is dying) the body of which should
have been a résumé of events since I last wrote. Yet my
letter was entirely taken up with one half hour spent in a
dilapidated bamboo-and-rattan shack with two old people
and their sick, mentally disabled son. It was the most pitiful
and deprived scene I had ever witnessed.

I was angry and frustrated with myself that all I could
do was converse with them in their own language and hand
over whatever pesos I had in my wallet. I came away with
the deepest admiration for the mother, the equal of Mother
Teresa, who was giving life to her two incapacitated men,
because the husband was bedridden with TB. This couple
are not legally married and the old lady wouldn't recognise
the inside of a church, yet I believe she is far more
Christlike than I.

Seamus has a point about opting out of institutional
Christianity. I hesitated to rejoice with him that he had

the courage to muscle his way out of that 'valley of dry bones'. I can't, and the why of it is muddled.

There is a part of me that's influenced by history. We are part of the Medicis, part of the Borgias. We hate our Church when it is narrow-minded; we love our Church because it is a big Church with room for all. I see myself as part of a historical institution, terribly human, full of laggards, saints, the fear-stricken, wobbling its way to great heights and terrible excesses of blindness.

If the day comes when that becomes unbearable because of the blindness element, I will not hang around any more; I will not mark time hoping and waiting for charismatic leadership.

But, right now, I cannot cut myself off from the likes of the Cathedral in Compostella, Bective Abbey (in ruins), my mother saying the rosary, the ritual (including incense) of a well-sung Gregorian Mass, and the faith many people still have in me.

Let's leave it at that. I never intended to rake this up, and I do want to get back to parts of your letter.

About four years ago, I wrote a full letter to Alice on what you now tell me is duality. Like you I discovered it for myself. The way I saw it at the time was that a person, in my eyes, became more perfect the more they could balance opposite virtues in themselves, such as patience and volatility, rigidity in the sense of having integrity and principles, and flexibility as expressed by compassion and understanding. It would be a person I'd be attracted to, because she (or he, in a different context) would never be a bore, never be too predictable.

What I've always feared in relationships is their

withering if the wadi becomes dried up, and there is no more searching and no more surprises. Marriage must be intolerable if that happens. If one goes to seed, how can the other not share the same fate?

Manila, 24 September 1975

I've neglected this letter because of the retreat. I had lost faith in conventional retreats, and what a surprise it was to participate in silence and reflection with a brilliant man who, after three talks, established a credibility with me that no retreat director had ever established before. He gave me a vision of Man, God, universe, Jesus Christ, salvation and evangelisation which peeled layers off the suffocating cocoon that time and a profusion of ideas and experiences had enmeshed me in. I see myself now sitting on a lone rock, in a bare landscape under a solid blue sky, not, as before, hacking my way through a jungle, with clearances here and there.

Annette, it's a wonderful thing to feel hope, to feel challenged, to realise all one has to do is get off one's arse and work with all one's might and creativity. Starry-eyed? No. I have to work harder, for longer, but whereas I was spread too wide before on unrelated matters, I am now back to a conviction about the living person of Jesus Christ from which all sorts of activities can radiate. This man helped me to give a real rather than notional assent to a few fundamental things in our faith. He was a real professional.

On the night the retreat finished, I ended up in, of all places, the British Club, complete with two-week-old copies of the *Telegraph* and a glowering painting of Winston in the foyer. The group-members were all a bit off the wall: Breda Brennan, the latest revolutionary among the Columban Sisters; Mary Radcliffe from Epsom; a revolutionary Filipino priest and nun recently released from jail, Louis Jalandoni and Connie Ledesma. The significant thing about them now, apart from their anti-Marcos pedigree, is that she is wearing a long dress, loose about the middle, and he is purring like a prospective father should. Both of them are highly talented and were active on behalf of the oppressed as priest and nun before martial law. They had to go underground after martial law, but were caught and ended up in jail. Now married, they appear to me to be another suburban couple, expecting a baby and heading for the very life which you have ambitions to extricate yourself from. Breda and Mary asked me after the meal why I was so silent. I felt sad, I said, and angry at our institutional Church for neutralising two fantastic people because they fell in love when the harassment in their lives was so great that they felt they needed one another permanently. And I felt angry with them, too, especially with him for abandoning his pulpit and leaving the job to ill-equipped men like me.

You said you could not understand celibacy. Here you would understand it less. But while it is there (and I'm not sure it's such a total disaster) guys like him and myself should put up with it – brave words which some day I hope I won't have to swallow!

If one opts out, the only alternative is suburbia, the school bus and the front lawn. A few times with Alice, the thought of it made me shiver.

172

I made known my views about Jalandoni's marriage to Pat Healy, another Columban who was up from Mindanao, not necessarily for the retreat. He tore strips off me. He's a bearded, tremendously alive Clareman who does not fit the bill of the institutional priest. His express purpose in being here, he said, was to undo the harm that has been done by four hundred years of Catholicism. He believes in Jesus, but says that the bible which is being written by the lives of people, mainly the oppressed, is more important than the Bible.

He roams around from one group of revolutionaries and oppressed to another He's committed to the overthrow of the Marcos government, and, like Jack Hynes, his actions are governed by the Marxist–Maoist analysis of society and politics. He's living with a very nice girl – not openly, though. He has the prophetic personality to get away with it. If I did that, I'd have superiors and bishops on my back all the time

I will mail this tomorrow, unfinished. I'll continue when I have some papers on missions readied for our forthcoming Columban Regional Convention.

Love, Jim

14

Today is 25 February 2002. Three more days and then this accursed month is gone, finished for another year. I'm very pleased with the progress I've made with Fat God, the computer filename now for my ego-boosting, twenty-five-years-of-life recording project .

At the beginning I set out a daily schedule for myself, because I had to. I had become a slob without an agenda. Breakfast at 9 AM. She gets up earlier and begins the day lightly on toast and marmalade, but eats and snacks regularly as the day goes on. I used to be the one who was always gaining weight. Now I'm losing it and she's gaining it. I have the full Irish (streaky rashers, of course) and one more solid meal before I go to bed. I am the chef for the solid meals, whereas the stir-fries with rice, *pancit*, *adobos*, etc. are her domain. We eat one another's cooking with impartiality.

After breakfast, I walk to the village. I usually feed the ducks in the Griffeen, a tributary of the Liffey which flows through the village and give it a focus. Clondalkin and Blanchardstown, sister towns, have no comparable focus. I buy the paper and do the Simplex crossword, which has become too simple, but it is an exercise which is a kind of governor on the quality of my recall and word power. I keep thinking about this senility thing and wondering when will I lose my marbles?

I work from 10.30 to 3 PM and then I do one or other of two

things. If it's my day to cook, I'm likely to choose home-cured bacon with cabbage and floury potatoes, which she and I lick our lips after – and our twenty-three-year-old student daughter and twenty-four-year-old worker son go to the fridge or the takeaway for an alternative menu. If it's not my day to cook, I take the cap off whatever Scotch I've bought and leave it off – there's no sense in fooling oneself. With the addition of ice and soda water, I enjoy a remarkably happy hour or two until I am nicely down the bottle.

I buy Haig, Teacher's, Whyte and Mackay or Stewart's Cream of the Barley, blended whiskies which are at a reasonable price in our two main supermarkets, Superquinn and Tesco. I never get a hangover from them, whereas wine's aftermath makes my head muzzy. After dinner, I go back to my Apple Mac to input what I've handwritten, to edit or to print out pages. Unless there's a soccer match or a good movie on, I'm in bed by 8 PM and I sleep like a log, even though I wake up for a pee around 3 AM.

Joe2's golf trip never got off the ground because his older brother, Father Tom, a Columban, died in the Bon Secours hospital in Dublin on Valentine's Day. He was waked in one of the front parlours in Dalgan Park. Herself and myself attended the wake and the funeral Mass and burial, next day. Tom was the seventh Columban, and the youngest, to die within the two months between 12 December 2001 and 14 February 2002. All were over seventy. There will be no replacements for them – from Ireland, anyway.

Tom had a generous and magnetic personality. It was he who invited me to join the group of oddbods at the British Club, Manila. He paid for the meal, too; none of us had much money and he was a member of the club because of his

175

apostolate among the English-speaking people in Malate. He had an unusual ability to communicate with left, centre and right, each of whom fraternised mainly among themselves.

By his bedside, and with his family during his last days was his friend, Margaret Healy, a nun of the St Louis Congregation and a sister of Pat, who tore strips off me in Manila. She mourned him too at the wake, and stayed by his open coffin. During the Mass, she read a lovely and enigmatic piece to us all from the pulpit. I hope her participation was more than a corporal work of mercy and compassion.

I hope she loved him and that he loved her too.

Some time during the eighties I met Jose Maria Sison again. He had been offloaded on me in Candelaria at the time that he was Philippines' Public Enemy Number One. I was told then that he was a Methodist missionary. The second time I met him, he had just been released from a long spell in jail and he and his wife were in Dublin, on their way to Holland, to join Louis and Connie Jalandoni, who were maintaining a European support-system for their faction in Filipino politics.

Jack Hynes and his Filipina wife, Lulu, threw a party for him and my wife and myself seemed to be the only non-left-wing guests present. What struck me that night was the reverence which all the guests had for him – awe, almost. I asked him a question or two about the revolution. I thought he would remember me from Candelaria. He didn't. He just looked at me, making me feel the outsider I was, said nothing and turned away. I turned to herself and said, 'Let's go home.'

Pat Healy, of course, and his Filipina wife, Nora, were there that night. Pat was drowned off west Clare in 1996. He had been working in a slate quarry, which was being run as a co-op, and Nora taught in a special school they and others with similar ideals founded, so that their children wouldn't be 'contaminated' by the Irish education system. Pat was a wild man, especially if he had drink on him. When he lost his driver's license he rode to town on a horse, and I was told that, on the occasion of one of his sprees, he rode the horse in the front door of the convent.

Joe2, Tony O'Dwyer, Donal McDonald's sister, Caroline, and myself went to the funeral among the limestone walls of the Burren. I was wondering how the parish priests would handle this hot potato and what could they say about Pat without putting their feet in it. I needn't have bothered. It was John Donoghue of *Anam Chara* fame who said the Mass and preached. It was a tour de force. He spoke of Pat as prophet and paid a great tribute to Nora as wife and mother. There were songs sung, tin whistles played, poems read and the most touching moment of all was when some man came to the microphone and just said, 'I loved him!'

When we went to Philippines in January, 2000 (she for the eighth time since we came home in 1977, and I for the first) it was the completing of the circle for me and the Columbans.

The buzz was gone.

The only voice crying in the wilderness came from Shay Cullen in his Preda fortress, north of Olongapo. He is without a doubt the most successful Columban self-publicist ever and his campaign against paedophilia is known worldwide.

I didn't visit him because I had too many crows to pluck with him and that would not be the way to revitalise a comradeship we had enjoyed almost forty years before.

I thought of the seventies in the Columban HQ on Singalong Street, Manila, when it was buzzing with anticipation at what was around the theology and missiology corners. None of us expected then that our hopes would be dashed by Rome.

Hynes and Healy, at that time, had the confidence of masters of the universe, and while we acknowledged their commitment and dynamism, most of us thought they had gone 'a bridge too far'. Yet theirs was a big improvement on evangelisation by numbers and holy water. It was some attempt at getting the *aggiornamento* show on the road.

My wife and myself were invited to Sunday-evening community dinner in Singalong and it was convivial. After twenty-three years' absence, I never missed a name, even though some of the guys had grown grey, or fat, or bald in the meantime. Columbans are pleasant enough people, whatever else I might say about them.

I returned by myself the following week to stay the night, with the view of having a bit of craic and a beer with the lads on the veranda, after supper, like old times. I sat there, alone, and nobody came. The spark lit by Roncalli had truly died. I said to myself, 'What the fuck am I doing here?' and went to bed.

At breakfast, next morning, I was joined by Dick Cannon who, as my last superior in Zambales, urged me to leave Santa Cruz and go to Candelaria, and by Peter Steen, the superior of the region of Philippines to whom I handed in my chips in 1977. It was 7 AM and I wanted to leave the place and join herself at the home of her sister, Nene Salud. I had only a five hundred peso note on me and I asked Dick, who was bursar, to break it for me for the taxi driver.

'The office will be open at 8 AM,' he replied, and left. Peter Steen broke it for me once Dick left.

Dick died while I was writing this, so *de mortuis nil nisi bonum*.

Since I'm filling gaps in the last chapter, left by time, Breda Brennan left the Columban sisters, and the last I heard of her was that she went for quality, married a Filipino monsignor, was living in Italy, and still fighting for causes. Mary Radcliffe is still a Columban sister. And from whom did I get an email during the week but the redoubtable Seamus, who is spending the winter months of his retirement in his apartment in Florida? They also have a house in New York.

He says in it: 'My father, although an atheist, was steeped in the Catholic tradition of work – by the sweat of thy brow, thou shalt earn thy bread. But, to him, work was a punishment to be avoided by all means possible. If a thorn bush stopped the cow going over the neighbour's ditch, he didn't bother with stake or wire. He never ploughed the headland or cut the hay in the corners with the scythe after the tractor had left. He spread the turf near the bog-hole and let the ass do the hauling when it was dry.

'He walked the bogs with his gun and put goose, duck, pheasant and grouse on the table several times a week He was not lazy, he did what had to be done and no more. And he worked his head.

'He got two small government jobs that took up a few hours a week but generated a cash flow: a half-crown for a copy of a birth certificate, ten bob for caretaking the dispensary, and the large sum of two pounds for being the presiding officer at election time – all probably the reward for being the founding member and main fixer of several Fianna Fáil cumainn in East Galway.

'I often think of him, especially when people ask me if I am really retired. A third believe I was put out to pasture. The telltale comment is: "I am sure you got a great package from Merck." A third believe that someone, still in his fifties, and moderately alert, must be bored out of his mind. Hence the phone call from the boss who gave me my first job in America. He is eighty-five, with a defibrillator and a pacemaker buried in his chest, and he is working on trying to get projects from the USAID money pouring into Afghanistan.

'"Now," sez he, "After two years, I am sure you want to get your teeth dug into something. Why don't you come back and take over IRI (International Research Institute)?"

'The third group, weighed down with an ethic of work and a Calvinist superego, would try to make me feel that there is something almost sinful in not "going to work". Like my father, I relish the time. I walk the beach, I listen to the news, I read and read and try to do a few small things to make some small spot in Africa a better place.

'Bored? I never knew the meaning of the word, and I hope I never will.

'Seamus'

15

Candelaria, 18 June 1975, 9.10 PM

Dear Mother Abbess,

I'm on the flat of my back under my mosquito net and very scantily clad – shamelessly uncovered, actually – to cope with the early humid, muggy days of the rainy season. I have the BBC World Service at my ear. It's 1.15 PM your time.

The musty smell of soggy clothes is in my nostrils and will stay there until September. Cloth and leather articles will have to get special attention, otherwise they'll rot. Mosquitoes multiply and invade the house. Bugs that jump and bang against the lights end up knocked out on the floor and the ants will be removing them by morning. The white ant is in the church. It concentrates on timber, and two days ago I found three nests of them, busily chewing up the *haligis* (timber pillars). I've got electric light now from 6 PM to 6 AM. Fabulous! I can read at night.

I'm room-fixing too, going to screen the windows so that I can throw this mosquito net out through one of them. It's like being in an oxygen tent. I hate it. You end up sleeping on the ashtray. Everything has to be in the bed. The pages of your June 4 are scattered all around me.

Your cure for boredom is like mine. How fantastic it would be, though, to have the friends we love available at least once a week, to affirm our flagging spirits, to fight and argue with us, to hug us and eat with us and tell us the truth.

You did Eleanor a great service by giving her a piece of your mind. I'm surprised you said that she'd have no choice about the abortion if she was pregnant and he wouldn't marry her. Why do you think she shouldn't live up to your standards? Should you soften a principle out of concern and a wish to tidy up loose ends? Eleanor's fast adoption of the standards of the world is an indictment of the kind of religious training she got. Could she possibly be psychologically prepared to leap into the sack with a man after a week or two out of the convent, or is it that she is a twit and in too much of a hurry to find a domestic life for herself? What has intelligence to do with being moral? Do those who are clear-sighted and mentally well-adjusted sin more? You have a strong streak of the Mother Abbess in you, but if I am to invest you with the mitre and crosier, you'll have to demand the same performance from your novices as you exact from yourself.

I don't feel protective towards women in general, but I would feel I had lost a limb if a few women I know were hurt, or hurt themselves. I guess I find my identity with them – Alice, you, Mary Foley, Anna Brady, Kitty O'Flaherty, Thu Thuy, Josefa Aldana. They don't fear me or play games with me, and they will probably feel sad when I die, and put flowers on my grave.

Seamus spoke about being rooted and grounded. I am happy with you and at home with you. Those few days with you brought back to me a buoyancy I only felt at eighteen, when I cut turf on a mountain and walked the heather with a lass with long black hair, who later married a man called Kennedy and died after her first childbirth.

I wrote to Alice last night, having got a nice letter from her yesterday. We seem to talk and think a lot about sex now. After six years of a John-of-the-Cross relationship, we're fast spinning down to earth. Is there a sex cycle in a love relationship which crowds out the normal interplay? Or is it that both of us are now at an age and a stage of the romance when the only dam still brimful is the passion one – bursting to be let loose and inundate the countryside?

How does one approach this passion in oneself? Do we just spend it? Mustn't there be some ritual with it? It's such a fantastic sacrament of giving. How do I know she won't be shattered psychologically by it? Stupid questions, I suppose, to which I don't expect an answer.

Imagine yourself being a nun for twenty years, and this event suddenly lets loose imprisoned yearnings, reflexes. What the hell would it do to you? Would it ever occur to you that it would be better to let sleeping dogs lie?

Seamus was right about the non-stimulating atmosphere of northern Zambales. The only thing I really find satisfaction in at the moment is the preparation and execution of my preaching. I cannot pray too well, I cannot administer or organise except in a fumbling way, but I do put all my enthusiasm into the Word of God. There's so much we can do if we get within range of people's thoughts and experiences. That determines what you say and how you say things.

The big crucifixion of the missionary is getting within range. Ask Seamus and he'll tell you how difficult it is for us Westerners to find the pulse and the nerve ends of the Oriental. Lao-tzu gives a wonderful insight into the uninvolved, passive man whom I meet so often. I'm wasting my time proposing a philosophy of action to him. I'll have to wrap it up in something else.

In most houses here, there are two figures or icons: Christ on the cross, and a flamboyant, Buddha-like porcelain statue representing prosperity and fertility. The latter is the more authentic idol for the Filipino, who does not feel guilt, and to whom self-abnegation on a permanent basis is crazy.

The most important criterion for me as a Westerner is reason. As a result, my actions are determined by my conscience. The Oriental's actions are determined by face. That leads to the question: if we have different cognitive processes, how the hell do we communicate? And that leads to another question – what the hell am I doing here anyway?

I swam but once off the beautiful beach of Libertador, just half a mile away. What a shame! I haven't that light-heartedness in me now. When I'm alone, I become dour. Backpackers are always welcome.

A girl from Berlin dropped by recently and stayed a few days. She was a 5' 10" leggy, blonde nurse, walking some of the quiet roads of Asia. She was infatuated with the beauty of northern Zambales and we got on well. One of the reasons she quit Berlin was that her husband, a Pole, was running around with some lassie who came west from Krakow and reanimated more than his nostalgia. She was awaiting a divorce, and although a Catholic, seemed to be unenthusiastic about anything the Church had to offer.

She was into reincarnation and tarot cards and stuff.

I should send her to you. God, would ye confuse one another!

You will make it to here some day. You've got to see the end of the world before you die, even if you do have some extra wrinkles here and there. If Seamus comes back, we'll start a fund.

I'm charmed you're happy with your new house. You are a romantic, you know, and are satisfied with very little. I never saw a house office, but if it inspires you to sit down and write, then I'm all for it.

Do I think the Protestant missionaries do better or worse by bringing their wives along? That depends on a lot of things – the calibre of the wife, the age of the children, the cultural adaptability of the whole family. It has to be a family vocation. For myself, I'd settle for a Seamus, a Heneghan, an O'Dwyer, an Eamonn O'Brien or a McKeating. I think I'd be afraid of marriage – anywhere. Best wishes to Miguel, Purita and Inigo.

Love, Jim

Candelaria, 31 July 1975

Dear Annette,

When I got your thick, juicy letter today, I read about two pages and then had to attend to some callers about a funeral. While I was talking to them, I was thinking (I do that regularly – carry on a conversation on one track while on another I'm having insights about something else) that when I read your letters, and yours alone, I feel grown up. Alice's are sometimes short, desperate, trying to express

185

the inexpressible. So are mine to her. I cannot be detached. The letters of Seamus are concise but comprehensive. J.W.'s are witty, readable and carefully tracked. I can't really explain why I should get that feeling from yours, but I do.

I'm in my boudoir, now screened and with a noisy, second-hand air conditioner. It's a luxury, I know, but I need it like I need love and affirmation – just to survive.

There's a gaping hole in the floor timbers through which I nearly disappeared a week ago, escaping with slightly injured *cojones* and straddling the joist which saved me. There was lurid language in the best Gaelic tradition, a deprivation which you English have to suffer on without. I remember you being shocked at the vocabulary of Seamus and myself, and since then I have been quite restrained in my language with you.

Your photograph has miraculously appeared beside another one of my parents on recently hammered-together bookshelves. For reasons only known to themselves, Thomas and Luz Morado (my cook, carpenter, fiscal and his wife, who is a religion teacher in the high school) chose it from a bunch of photos, put it in a frame and there it was. It was the picture of you in green, about which my mother is reported to have said, 'Who is that woman?'

Remember you sent it to me so that I would recognise you at Heathrow, and it didn't arrive in time. I had instructed Mother to open any letters which came for me after I left. Mother is too much of a lady to read anyone's letters, but she couldn't avoid seeing the photo. She confided to my sister, though, that she'd only be 'nervous of the nuns'. Two of my Dalgan classmates married nuns after ten years in the priesthood and she knew them well.

Alice has visited her and I suspect my mother was damn glad to see me leave Ireland still wearing the Roman collar. I also suspect Alice has told her the score, and if she hasn't, Mother will have read between the lines.

I'm going to bed. Good night. You're smiling at me from your newly framed picture.

PS Out here one can come very close to dying of loneliness. In that state, nothing matters except not to cause pain to someone else. One is living at the extremes and there are times all one sees is the futility of making any lasting contribution. One is on a wagon train to nowhere.

1 August

A good job I stopped there. My pessimism was welling up. It is very important in life to see the sad and futile side of things too, in order to keep one from being a pie-in-the-sky idiot. I fluctuate between one state and the other. I have no steady temperament – a bit like yourself! People like us should never live together. What would happen if our moods synchronised? We'd either blow the slates off with gaiety and exuberance, or spend the day playing Russian roulette. And our children would all be schizophrenic.

Thanks for what you said about my writing. Once in a while I feel I'm saying things that are really mine, but from lack of discipline they end up fragmented and weak.

'A more useful and relevant occupation when the children are older?' Say in fifteen years' time, when you're pushing fifty. I bet five pounds you won't move a leg. Have

187

your dreams anyway. I think you're great *now*. George Elliot of Norwich told Seamus that the only place for a Westerner is in the West. So, you're only teaching Spanish. So, I'm only teaching the penny catechism. It's the personal vibrations in us that cause change. I swear I'd be far more effective in your school than I am here.

There is a confusion, spiritual starvation, dehumanisation in Europe that is whispering to me to go back and work among people in a way the unliberated, institutionalised priests can't or won't. I think that, now more than ever before, the priesthood is relevant, whether it's your kind or mine.

There must be people who can survive and act as Christians – simple, well-adjusted, happy contradictions to a way of life that is becoming more tinselled and dehumanising. They never carry placards or wear insignia, but they are good news at a party, on the street or in a school staffroom. There's a constancy and transcendence about them in a world of quick change and uncertainty. There's a courage about them, in an age of captivities and arse-licking. They're low-key, like Nathaniel in the Gospel. They go out of their way, break conventions with sangfroid and are an advert for unselfishness.

Who the hell wants to be a nun with opportunities like that around?

I thank you for your letters. They mean a lot. Reading them and replying gives me a chance to get away from baby talk, to rummage in my depths for what's left of my consciousness. I'll dry up if I find myself singing the same song.

Your essay on love and sex in one's thirties was quite

beautiful. I take your word for it. I'll be forty-one next month, and Alice will be thirty-eight on her next birthday. Age is of no consequence to us. May God keep us all alive until '79. I wish for nothing else.

7 August

I had a meeting tonight with six of the *mulier fortis*-type women in the parish about an envelope system for the Sunday collection through which I'm getting about nine pounds per month. One of the six is more *mulier* than *fortis*, a virgin in the statute books, built like a model, thirty-ish and putting the 'come hither' on me. Thomas Aquinas would scourge himself with nettles, St Kevin would heave her over a cliff in Glendalough, but since I am the Sir Lancelot type, I'll just stand my ground and see what happens. It's all good clean fun!

Love, Jim

Candelaria, 4 December 1975

Dear Annette,

I got back from Manila this afternoon knowing there would be a letter from you – and there was. I was relieved to learn that you received the gewgaws because I had reservations about deceiving Her Majesty's postal services by concealing them in a cassette-tape case. Anyway, I'm glad you liked the silver pendant, crafted in Baguio, Philippines.

I went to Manila to find a person with a certain background, a certain competence and a certain vision of the future whom I want to work with me in the creation of and use of audiovisuals (slides or filmstrips) for evangelisation. Carolyn doesn't have the time or the professionalism. I sifted the sands and found a woman, an ex-newspaper journalist turned *madre* who has training in AV and communications, and all I've to do is convince her top brass that living and working with Kennedy will bring the Kingdom of God quickly and effectively to Candelaria. I didn't meet her but was tipped off about her by a well-known member of the same congregation, Sister John Patrick, a friend of many Columbans, whom I visited because I was told she was a mine of information. I had gone to the Daughters of St Paul, who specialise in media, but drew a blank.

I met Rosella, too, and had to give her my portable typewriter to work on term papers – which leaves my station here now with one wobbly 1904 Underwood.

I was in Manila for three days and got a total of eight hours' sleep. It's where one meets people, and after being cooped up here for months, I was exposed to cross-currents from different groups and people.

Are we just maintaining parishes or building Christian communities? Should we be involved primarily with the poor? Should we openly fight oppression, even if it is perpetrated by the President? If we're making a lifelong commitment to the Philippines, could we be better adjusted and culturally more acceptable if we married Filipinas? Stuff like that.

I believe the Roman Church is wrong in this age not to give her priests a free choice of marriage or celibacy. I believe the same choice should be available to women when, in the future, they will become priests.

I believe many priests and nuns are not cut out for the non-married life, but I do believe there are men and women who can live as what you call 'normal human beings' without the companionship and fulfilment of marriage. If many priests are 'incredible' and live such 'odd lives', it's not because celibacy is wrong, but because celibacy as a general rule is wrong. Christ, Francis of Assisi, John of the Cross, Thomas Merton all had the ability. Mother Teresa has it. If the lonely, isolated life warps and cripples a man or woman and doesn't liberate them to pursue their ideals and a more intense and widespread apostolate, then it's the wrong choice.

When I said previously that marriage is a higher and more demanding vocation, I'm not just quoting myself. Any theologian of any standing would back me. I will not give up this place, though. I've no doubt that in twenty or thirty years, some priest will bring his wife in here but he will do it because I've stayed here, not because, at forty-one, I have started a new life in some European suburb and fulfilled the deep physical and emotional longings within myself.

The ultimate meaning of the Cross is that in a crunch we are called upon to destroy ourselves if the motives are good enough. Life can be 'normal' if it fits in with what you believe to be God's plan for you.

What I'm saying is that, in the current structures, when we need all the guts and sanctity we've got to topple some mediaeval gods, the place to fight the battles is from within. In a battle you sacrifice pawns first, not knights and castles. The laity can do nothing about it, because the Church is not a democracy.

I'm letting this off to you but I can't help it. Christmas is a mad time and I must put a lot of work into ten slide sermons for the *Misa de Gallo*, which runs to packed churches in Candelaria at 4 AM every morning from 16 December to 25 December.

Love, Jim

Candelaria, 29 January 1976

Dear Annette,

It's the cool of the evening. I'm sitting in my favourite wicker chair upstairs. Somebody is sweeping the yard, and the soothing, regular strokes of the coconut-fibre brush are coming up mingled with the shouts of children playing in the plaza. I'm drinking a shot of Anejo rum, having been converted to it by circumstance. It is eight pesos per pint bottle (twenty pesos to the pound), whereas Scotch is fifty to eighty pesos per pint. I like my little *deoch,* and sometimes I ask myself whether I like it too much – an irrelevant question because, as with love, I'm not going to give it up.

Today we had a retreat for all 150 of our second-year students. First-years were 'renewed' ten days ago. For quiet, I took them out to a small island in the delta of a local river, hoping I would make them feel some kind of religious experience. But between worrying about them getting drowned and a daylight screen which failed to reflect filmstrips, I didn't repeat it, and kept Second Year on the compound.

These evangelical events tire me like hell because I can't parrot clichés. Every time I 'prophesy', my beliefs

Vising during the making of the audiovisual presentation *Fat God, Thin God*, 1976.

Jim with farmers in Candelaria, taking pictures for use in audiovisual pre-sentations.

Vising at the railway siding in Damortis, on the way to Baguio with Jim, May 1977.

The wedding portrait taken on 7 July 1977, Manila, Philippines.

Jim and Vising with her parents, Vicenta and Regalado, photographed at Manila Airport before leaving for Ireland, 12 September 1977.

Jim and Vising Kennedy, Lucan, County Dublin, 13 September 1977.

Jim with his son, Patrick, in 1978 in Lucan, County Dublin.

Vising, Patrick and Noriana holidaying in Rosses Point, Sligo in 1983.

Regalado, Vising's father, on his visit to Ireland in 1982 with Nora, Vising's mother-in-law, Mary Mills, her sister-in-law, Pat and Nan (the children) and John Mills.

The Kennedys on Patrick's Communion day in May 1985.

Annette Rowland

Jim chewed the stems of many pipes during his years at Smurfit Publications.

Jim with Seamus Connolly, taken in Lucan, County Dublin, 1990.

Joe (Joe2) and Teresa O'Grady-Peyton showed great loyalty to
Jim, and vice versa.

The 'Legion of Mary meeting': Jim and his friends in Courtney's pub in
Lucan for their regular Sunday lunchtime rendezvous.

Jim and Vising with three examples from their bonsai collection, at home in Lucan.

Jim enjoying his retirement in 2000.

come echoing back to me for confirmation. Today I made a pleasant discovery about my least qualified catechist.

I have four who were here when I came: one nun, two mature women who spent two years in catechetical school, and this one, Lea Fomera. For some reason, she failed to make the grade in catechetical school and was let go after one year. I took the four of them aside after the recollection day of the first-years and told them it was not information the kids needed, but a message which should spring from their own convictions.

'Less of the script,' sez I, 'and more of yourself.'

This lass let herself go today, and it appears to me that she has more fire and personal conviction than the other three together. She was brilliant and I can't help but give myself a modest pat on the back for triggering off something. I believe a major part of the job here is to be a catalyst, to be able to spot and encourage talent in those around us. I could never achieve what she did today in a million years. If I was your parish priest, I'd have you preaching the Word in some shape or form too.

30 January, morning

I fell asleep on the job last night and having reread your December diary, which I got early in January, I have some explaining to do. I ended up in hospital after an utterly exhausting but vibrating Christmas.

On 26 December, when I was flattened after pouring myself out in a nine-day frenzy of mission, two nurses and a teacher from Mayo arrived and stayed four days. They were friends of Kieran Heneghan, who threw a party for them in

Olongapo when they arrived. Heading the Columban entertainment were Frankie and Barney, who are good singers and good craic and keep needling one another. Barney's most notable needle to Frankie was, 'Sing another song, Kelly, and depress me more.'

The three girls were just holidaying, looking for a suntan to face the west of Ireland again during the corpse-white months of January and February. They were nice people in their thirties, but were a bit stunned by it all. One of them became rigid at the sight of the small lizards running upside down across the ceiling, so I plied her with altar wine – the only anaesthetic I could lay my hands on – and it cured her, but depleted my stock and I couldn't say Mass.

Then my car conked out and I had to have it towed the ninety miles south to Olongapo to a mechanic who charged me 750 pesos to have it mended. I towed the Irishwomen too, and on the way down met a lively group coming up from Manila to stay with me for a week. All I could say to them was, 'Jesus Christ, when is Christmas going to end? I have no bed sheets, and the food and drink is gone.'

The group was made up of two American-born priests, a Franciscan and a Columban, and three nuns, all Filipinas.

'Trust the Lord, Jim,' they said, and sped north, where they intended to spend a lot of time on Libertador beach.

Things worked out well. The necessities came from somewhere and we laughed a lot. I felt like the guy in the spaghetti western who, lying half-scalped and arrow-pierced, was asked if it hurt. 'Only when I laugh,' he replied.

Since Christmas day, I had a continual pain in my stomach and I was thinking: here it comes, the first ulcer or cancer from the fifty cigarettes a day. After the visitors departed, I drove to Manila, had a complete check-up and emerged without flaw. I was just worn out and psyched up, as was proved when I slept round the clock for two days. I'm game ball again.

Your letter of 13 to 16 January reflected a new mood of calm and assurance – however long it will last. You can never resist stirring the sh—! You do seem to be experiencing the ideal – living in harmony with yourself, nature and God.

I don't have a woman in the house. I'm still negotiating for her, and if and when she does come, she will stay in the convent with the other nuns. She is a specialist in her congregation, St Paul de Chartres, who also run the school here. She edits the Congregation's paper, helps out with their mass-communications programme and has just completed a month-long seminar on audiovisuals. It is a bit of a step down for her to come here, so someone down there in Manila has a bit of initiative and adventure to release her. I am becoming more and more convinced that we have to begin at the perimeter, where human problems are greatest, and work inwards. There are too many people concentrated in central institutions, compounding the problems of education, development and evangelisation.

Anyway, if she does come, I won't have her in the house. Satisfied? Here the greatest deprivation is good communication, and if it turns out that I can communicate with her like I can with you, then the intensity of it and the sheer need of it magnifies, and in no time we become lovers, simply because the background is so abnormal.

The relationship I have with Alice and the understanding and affection that exists between you and me are normal and reliable. Here I am in a hothouse, and too many oppressions and deprivations make any love-relationship suspect. It could be a crutch to get over the bad patches.

By the way, Alice is up the creek again and wouldn't write because she didn't want to give me an earful of her woes. She's efficient, responsible and very human in her job as provincial bursar, a post she assumed since I returned to the Philippines. She is an automatic choice as representative for many other extra-curricular functions. She went into a spin when one of her contemporaries in the convent let bitchiness get the better of her and made remarks to the effect that Alice was 'a glamour girl, seeking out notoriety'.

The fact that a contemporary could be so bitter made her want to resign and hide herself as a classroom teacher again. Alice grew through affirmation and trust. She has this thing about betrayal and considers it the biggest sin of all. It is an aberration in her, because betrayal is somebody else's problem and the betrayed shouldn't allow it to infect them too. Anyway, she was saved by the bell – she passed her driving test and got the thing out of her system by careening around alone in the new car which goes with the job.

Spain in 1979, or early 1980? Seamus should be available to be summoned from wherever he is. I suspect there's no hope of dragging Alice along, unless the institution and her conscience could be outwitted. Rubbing shoulders with real life would really help her, though.

I heard from Seamus too. No, I don't worry about him. The direction of his life and his works indicates his faith and I join with you in praying that another kind of faith in God will replace what he seems to have lost.

I did laugh at your concern over the extra wrinkle. When I saw you, almost a year ago, you had the complexion of one of Robin Hood's mistresses, the figure of a lass out of a Sunday supplement and the verve of a sixteen-year-old. Have you fallen to pieces since?

An intimate revelation from Alice last July proves women have similar preoccupations. It gave me a great lift.

It was an observation of hers after a day swimming in Lough Sheelin: 'I know I've turned thirty-eight but my breasts are still firm.'

What implication that revelation has for me remains to be seen. Maybe there is a heaven after all!

Love, Jim

16

On reading my written words about the *Misa de Gallo* Christmas routine in Candelaria twenty-five years later, I couldn't quite recall the atmosphere there. The event that came to mind was my first Christmas Mass in Subic. It blew my mind, first with shock and then with pleasure.

It came as a big surprise to me that the 'aircraft hangar' would be packed, with a sizeable spillover outside the doors, whereas on Sundays throughout the year it was never full. St James's Church had neither steeple nor bell, so from speakers on the roof, pointed at the four corners of the parish, poured Christmas carols so loud I jumped out of bed at 3 AM on 16 December 1971 and rushed to ask, 'What the hell's going on?'

'We want the parishioners to be here at four,' Romy Maningding answered calmly. 'This is how we wake them up, because there are no alarm clocks in Subic.'

Filipinos are impervious to loud music, as the younger generation of Irish are to ear-bashing disco music, and while I have very sensitive hearing, I went along with it; I couldn't afford alarm clocks for the parish. When 4 AM arrived, the carols were mercifully turned off, and the singing in the church, accompanied by guitars and castanets, began.

It was magic; it was moving; it suited the occasion. Very rarely, when you're up there in white robes, are you uplifted by the congregation. You're usually thinking about what can go wrong. The uplifting came from below this time, and for once I thought to myself that it was indeed a great pleasure to be at an event while something wonderful was happening.

Filipinos in general don't go in for 365-days-a-year religion or 52-weeks-a-year religion. They do go in for 15-days-a-year religion – Easter (five days), Christmas (nine days), the town fiesta (one day) – and when they celebrate them, they do it in style. Philippines has great repertoires of folk music and dance, which still need a Filipino Sean Ó Riada and Michael Flatley to reinterpret and revitalise them.

Herself was within a month of giving birth when she attended her first midnight Mass in Ireland. It was in Lucan, in 1977. She had to stand. In the light of what we were used to, it was as dull as ditchwater.

The Irish know how to celebrate. We are good at integrating music, song and dance as events. Yet the Irish Church was years behind the Third World when it came to the stage management of religious emotions. Once in a while, in disagreement over something with Seamus, the epitome of the Aristotelian man, I used to say, 'Less reason, please, Seamus; more emotion and more instinct.'

The Irish missionary experience in Asia, Africa and Latin America will be a footnote in the history of how we handled culture. We will rank high in our contribution to education and health care, but what cultural goodies did we recognise out there, not to mention bring back home to our seminaries and churches? What music, what song, what dance, what literature for our magazines? The answer is zilch. Up until now, that is.

Filipina dancers, doing the *Pandanggo sa Ilaw*, provided the pièce de résistance at the Christmas Midnight Mass at St Mary's

Church, Lucan, in 2001. Why? Because Filipino nurses are here in their hundreds, and because herself, a cog in the parish machine, wants to heat things up à la Philippines. High time. And à la Peru too, and Chile and Jamaica and Nigeria . . .

Joe2 is in the business of recruiting labour forces from one country to work in another. It so happens that his company has played a significant role in the placement of Filipino nurses in Irish hospitals and health care centres. Part of that role is in the provision of a substantial cultural-orientation course, for the Filipinos as well as the receiving hospitals, which after two years in existence is beginning to show dividends.

Four thousand or more Filipinos have come to work in Ireland, over the past two years especially. This is the biggest ethnic migration into Ireland since the coming of the Normans in the twelfth century and the plantation of Ulster in the seventeenth century. Joe2 knew it would have to be managed properly, because, like myself, he lived and worked in Philippines too, so he commissioned herself and myself to develop a series of briefings which would help the newly arrived workers to adjust quickly and to integrate into Irish society, rather than live on the fringes, with the possibility of being ghettoised at some time in the future.

Maybe my seven years in Philippines, which I considered a waste, weren't such a waste after all.

Four Columbans came back to Ireland between 1977 and 1979 with Filipinas as wives. Jack Hynes had Lulu Ledesma, a young widow with seven children. Pat Healy had Elenora Lim, and the first of their four boys, Dante (named after the NPA leader, Buscayno, whose alias was Commander Dante). Hilary Shannon had Veronica Castaniego, and I had herself. We kept in close contact for the first few years, and ran into other Irish guys married to Filipinas, like Tony O'Hanlon, a flour-miller in Pasig, Manila, where he met and married Esther Bernadas, and Pat Keating, a PR consultant, who met Nita Sebastian in Rome. We had little to celebrate about, job-wise, but we came together at the drop of a hat, and the group kept on widening.

The girls would cook up a storm out of nothing, and I could soon see that thirty or forty guests were, for them, as easily handled as five. That was the culture they brought with them. The Irish husbands were indulged and allowed to talk about their glorious pasts in the tropics while sampling many off-licence brands with impartiality.

Out of those get-togethers grew the Filipino–Irish Association, which now has its own constitution and six hundred members. Herself was first chairperson of the Association. Its main purpose was to offer an opportunity to Filipinos, anywhere in Ireland, to come together at least once a year, meet their fellow countrymen and countrywomen, and celebrate like they do in Philippines.

The O'Sullivans heard about it through some grapevine in west Mayo and arrived in on top of us the night before one of those pre-Christmas parties. Sean was from Ballycroy, and Florita, his tall and beautiful wife, was from the province of Antique, in the Visayas. They had five children, ranging in age from about three years old up to ten. Until the grapevine message was intercepted, Sean thought he was the only Irishman married to a Filipina in Ireland, and Florita thought she was the only Filipina in Ireland. They met one Sunday after Mass in Ballycroy and Sean decided, after years of dallying, that she was the one.

I began talking about our marriage and the cultural hiccups that had occurred in the relationship, which had to be thought through. Florita would look at Sean once in a while with a kind of 'I told you so' look in her eyes. It hadn't occurred to either of them that their Catholicism wasn't the sole glue keeping them together, that their different cultures and different cognitive processes would be a cause of mis-understandings which would have to be considered and resolved outside of Mother Church. They had coped brilliantly, though, and were glad of the night-long revelations and discussion which enriched all of us.

Tragically, Florita died suddenly from an aneurysm in the brain four years later, leaving the eldest, Luzviminda (Mindy), to assume the role of little mother to the other four. That tragedy in their lives was redressed a little five years later, during the happy days when Mindy became perhaps the most popular Rose of Tralee ever.

It is 5 March, and the snow and ice haven't come yet. I have fewer than ten chapters to go, and most of the material in them is contained in the letters. Herself proof-reads the chapters and offers advice, which I don't take. She has a different mind to me. She likes to gnaw at paragraphs, and suggests other options, whereas all I'm interested in is getting it all out of me and down on paper in any shape or form. I write like I used to play golf – by walking up to the ball and hitting it without thinking. That's the way I wrote the letters to Annette in the first place.

There's an episode in letters coming up which has a lady called Mena Escriva Garcia, and herself is unhappy with it.

'Why is it bugging you?' I asked.

'People will think you were a *palikero* then,' she said.

A *palikero* is a Philippine version of a G. B. Shaw, Irish

202

philanderer. I'm astonished that she would even conceive of associating the word '*palikero*' with me. I have never, consciously or unconsciously, manipulated women. A philanderer is a manipulator. I took women seriously and treated them as equals. The sexual-attraction factor had never seriously disturbed my relationship with women, but it began to do so at a time when I thought age (forty-two) and wisdom would make things easier. Far from it. I was now giving some women a second look, something I had never done before. It was as if there was some *dúchas* in myself which had either been suppressed or concealed for twenty-five years, and suddenly it wanted to express itself.

I believe now that it was the '*briseann an dúchas trí shúilimh an chait*' syndrome which kicked in and effectively guided me, instead of my priestly intentions. The phrase, an old saying in Irish, can be roughly translated as 'nature breaks out through the eyes of a cat'. Instinct was triumphing over the reason of St Thomas Aquinas, and *dúchas* – which means one's nature, genetics, the tribal paraphernalia which doesn't even get a mention in André Comte Sponville's eighteen virtues – was taking over my 'higher' aspirations.

The Kennedy men are late developers. My father was thirty-eight when he married, because the *dúchas* didn't hit him until then. He was a sportsman, kept himself busy with the Black and Tans, and had a Bridget O'Sullivan for every Thu Thuy I had, but one day he got nailed. I knew then that one day I was going to get nailed, and the one thing I had to be sure of (like him) was that it wasn't going to be a haphazard selection. I knew the crunch was coming and that it would happen whether I liked it or not. Two irreconcilable forces were speeding towards a head-on collision, and the one that would win was *dúchas*. The one that would lose was my continuing isolation in the priesthood from the common man, and most especially from the common woman. I knew that in my gut then, but I didn't know when it would happen, or with whom.

That was a terrible state to be in. I didn't realise I was going through some sort of mid-life crisis which had to do with my mind, my emotions and my heterosexuality. Up to this, my training as a priest had the major influence in the way these three performed for me. At forty-two, a *dúchas* which had been sleeping for twenty years woke up and began to seriously influence my mind (I was having reservations about the quality of my life – even my intellectual life), my emotions (this stuff going on with Alice, Thu Thuy and Annette was symptomatic of a deep need in me) and my heterosexuality, which I know now was out of shape because of ignorance and guilt, and which pointed back to the flawed presentation of people's sexuality in the seminary. The very fact that the classes were known as *De Sexto et de Nono* (concerning the Sixth Commandment – 'Thou shalt not commit adultery' – and the Ninth – 'Thou shalt not covet thy neighbour's wife') showed that morality, not biology or psychology, was at the heart of the dialectic about sex for the priest as well as the people. I talked to Annette recently about this and asked her for an honest answer to the question of how I had seemed to her then in my attitudes to women and sexuality.

'You were a complete ignoramus,' she answered bluntly.

17

Candelaria, Good Friday, 1976

Dear Annette,

This evening I'm going to talk about the small people of the world – the orphans, the haggard wives, the unemployed, the underpaid, the undernourished – who, like Christ, are crucified by the Herods, the Caiaphases, the Pilates and the vacillating, expediency-minded mobs who chose Barabbas. The greatest temptation of Christ must have been to remain up there when they taunted him, 'Come down from the cross and prove you are God!'

Implicitly we hear that taunt nowadays, but it's directed at the Third World, at the helpless sugar worker: save yourself. Christ wouldn't and didn't. The sugar worker cannot. The Arabs saved themselves with oil, but the crucified wife – can she? Or the landless and waterless – can they? Jurgen Moltman, a contemporary Lutheran theologian, has written a very interesting book called *The Crucified God*, which, for me, has thrown a new light on the meaning of the cross in our Christianity.

Anyway, how are you? Since I haven't heard from you in a while, are you having a love affair or something?

On Easter Monday I escaped to the mountains of Baguio, where we have a house. I stayed for a week. I brought an old priest with me, and three female teachers from the public elementary schools of Candelaria (aged twenty-nine, twenty-seven and twenty-four) with whom I've a sort of easy rapport. They stayed with friends. The aged-twenty-nine lady is the *mulier fortis* who was putting the 'come hither' on me. She has remained in Candelaria out of filial duty to aged parents. She is incredibly beautiful, which is one reason why she doesn't have a man in her life. 'They are afraid of me,' she explained.

It was the first time I ever heard of beauty victimising the beautiful.

I rounded up two young Columbans, found a respectable place where there was a nice combo, and we all danced flat out. The lads took to temptation like ducks to water, and, give me my due, I divided my dancing talents equally among the three teachers.

I enjoyed it immensely because I prize normality more than 'priestliness' and I love to see the virtues of enthusiasm and vivaciousness being exercised. Maybe that was part of Christ's package deal: 'I come that you may have life and have it more abundantly.'

Your monthly covenant (that's what the boys in Solihull call it) is coming through after a temporary stoppage. From May 1975 to April 1976, one hundred pounds has been received and spent. I put Rosella through a drama workshop for two months, and with her board and lodging included, the cost was forty-five pounds.

I have the horrible job now of making up the parish

and school financial statement for the last year. *I hate it.*

Jim

Candelaria, 30 April 1976

Dear Annette,

My last to you was hardly on the road to Manila when yours arrived. You are a very faithful woman indeed, and I understand the frame of mind you spoke of, which left you too unsettled to write. You analyse and explain your feelings very well. I hope Seamus visited you. I got word indirectly that he had been in New York and was sick, so I'm damned if I know what to think. We were and are the best of friends, but the fates seem to be working diversely in both of us now – he's becoming more sceptical and I'm becoming more and more convinced and concerned about Christianity.

I hope this does not cause any fundamental change in our friendship. He is faithful, and is so scrupulously conscientious he will always remain a Christian in spirit.

Charles, your priest friend, is not in my league at all. He must be Anglo-Saxon. He has no poetry in him. He must be what they call a churchman. In a way, I admire him for not having the vulnerability I'm tormented with so often. He will probably become a canon or a bishop, because he can detach himself from emotion.

It struck me recently, as I drove along somewhere – what special concessions will be awarded on the day of judgement to the man with a scrotum full of unused semen, and to the woman with the unshattered hymen?

You ask if love is a waste of time, especially if it doesn't bring about some sort of parousia for one. I don't regret

207

the many shapes and forms in which it has visited me. I've never been scorned or rejected. I do admit to being a bit of a Scarlet Pimpernel – not out of choice, but because it goes with the job. In a real crunch, I would not back off a genuine relationship because of some expediency.

Alice was able to write recently: 'I'm not afraid any more if you fall in love with someone else; it will be mild and you will come back to me.' She's right for one big, basic reason: the nitty-gritty of humdrum life without frills could be lived with her, because of our common culture and long understanding. She's not as provocative as you, as mysterious as Thu Thuy, as beautifully transparent as Josefa, as dynamic as Anna and as gently loving as Kitty. Children? The thought never entered my mind. The responsibility is too awesome for someone of my scattered outlook and uncertain future.

10 May

The weather is so hot that my brain is becoming anaesthetised, as well as my body. That's why tropical religion has more anaesthetic in it than catharsis.

You raise an interesting point about wanting to be happy only in a simple way. That is an illusion of yours, a pipe dream. You have an attractive demon in you which incites you to take that extra step which no simple person, going their simple ways, would dream of taking. You screw up the simple life by reaching out and probing and dreaming. The simple life is a Utopia I bypass every day, because I find some stone I haven't upturned or some roof I haven't brought crashing down around my ears.

My ideal finds a sympathetic chord in Picasso's attitude to painting. He's supposed to have said, 'If you're clear in your mind about what you're going to paint, there's no sense in painting it.' Our work should always be uncovering surprises, new options, new necessities. We should gear ourselves to life so that its Pandora's box confronts us, teases us, frightens us, awes us and shocks us into becoming bigger and better, albeit a bit more furrowed.

I just loved your fantasy of striding up the middle aisle to the altar, in anger, and flinging everything to the ground, taking your clothes off and scattering them on the ground too. How in the name of God could a women with fantasies like that live a simple life?

By the way, if you ever get round to making a reality of your fantasy, make sure you lock up the sacristan first. Part of his job is to be on the lookout for crazy women who have a compulsion to strip in front of the tabernacle.

Next month I'm finally going to get down to real work, with the coming of my prima donna, Vicenta Benavidez. If we click, we can set this place on fire. If she starts saying, obediently, 'Yes, Father', 'No, Father', I'm done. I told you about her, I think. She's a nun, an ex-journalist and news photographer turned evangelist, and her forte now is adult-formation and family-life enrichment. She is not as film-starish as my dancing partner in Baguio, Mena Escriva Garcia, and not as tall. Thank God for small mercies.

I'm at a dangerous stage in life. Sometimes I feel like a rhinoceros, caged away from water, and on the brink of smashing the bars to smithereens to get down there and wallow. I don't have a sense of discipline or order, only a kind of conscience, which serves the same purpose as the umbrella for the clown in the trapeze act.

Keep your heart up. If you believe in me, believe you have one friend for the nitty-gritty. I'm glad you got through that cloudy patch and found the sunlight. Nice, too, to see Bethany on your letterhead. I'm thinking of calling my place Gethsemane. People say they go through the wringer here. Regards to the three musketeers.

Love, Jim

23 May 1976, 7.30 PM

Dear Annette,

I'm writing by flickering candlelight, and not one of those fat candles we use in Ireland, but a thin little bugger that lasts but a half-hour and has to be replaced. The second typhoon is passing over, and the electricity is off. Internationally the typhoons have names like Olga, Pamela and so on. Here we Filipinise them. Last week's sweetie, Didang, scared the hell out of me in Manila as I drove through two and a half feet of water (accurate measurement) in my Volks after being marooned for two days in someone's house. By the grace of God and the ingenuity of the Volkswagen's manufacturers, I got through on the watery slipstream of a truck. Now I'm listening to Eding. They're named alphabetically as they arrive, so E (for Eding) being the fifth letter of the alphabet, this is the fifth typhoon so far. The next trollop will probably be Francing. That's just background. What's on my mind is this.

I'm in turmoil. It's a woman. I'm telling you because I've learned to tell you things like this. You may find it

210

odd that you are the first one I think of telling, and, perhaps, the only one. I can pretend to be asking your advice, but I'm not. I want your reaction. I'll give myself the advice.

This is the story.

I told you about the girl whom I thought beautiful, Mena Escriva Garcia. We danced all night up in the mountains, and I circumspectly shared my clumsy dancing with all three girls. There was static between me and Mena. One feels that intuitively. Once, while I was changing gears, she did not remove her knee. She asked me questions the others wouldn't normally ask.

They live a very staid life here, those girls, so we planned another trip up to a mining camp, Acoje Mines, where a friend of mine is chaplain. The idea was to picnic and swim in a river that flows through the jungle and is accessible only by a logging road. We did just that, adding two male teachers to the group, and had a whale of a time. The static was getting worse between Mena and myself, yet there was nothing explicit or determined between us. We talked about people and each of us knew we were talking about ourselves.

Here I have to give you her background. Middle-class family, college-educated. Has all the units necessary for an MA but hasn't written her thesis. As a college student aged twenty-two, she got engaged, and that lasted four years. She wanted to marry the guy, but the parents kept stalling and eventually pulled her out of Mindanao, where she was studying, and brought her back here. Parents can be very unreasonable if they need one member of the family to look after them (she's the youngest). The guy came here, but *pietas* determined the issue, so he went off and married someone else. At present there's an engineer dying to marry her, but she's just not interested.

I felt that if the build-up of whatever was between us wasn't broken, the tension would become unbearable. So I broke it with a letter telling her the truth. We were putting our heads in a sack because I couldn't offer her marriage. I could love her, but it would be conditional and therefore I shouldn't try. Deep down, I didn't know her or her people from Adam, but emotionally and sexually she was on my mind all the time.

She replied very honestly, remembering things we had contrived, almost unconsciously, to keep the flame going. She said she was in love and accepted my evaluation of things. I suggested that we had to talk about this, so that there would be no illusions.

That in itself was an illusion.

She was supposed to meet me in Manila, but because of the typhoon floods I only reached the street where she was staying (walking in a foot of water) in time to go home. She said she would come home with me and we could talk on the way.

Storm signal number three was up and I talked about everything of relevance I knew. She listened and said little. Then I held her hand and the passion and tension was there. She wasn't listening any more. She was just waiting. The darkness came, the rains got worse, the wind blew harder. I had to pull off the road, and that let loose a typhoon within a typhoon.

Never in my wildest dreams could I have imagined a woman so hungry for love. In cries and moans and words in some Filipino language I didn't know, she said what she couldn't have said in a thousand words. I responded to her hunger, because there was a terrible hunger in myself too. After an hour or so in the impossible front seat of the VW, and without a garment being displaced (disturbed, yes) we went home drained and airily happy. All the tension had gone.

That's where it's at now. I cannot see her here. Traditions are as archaic in Candelaria as they were in Victorian England. Rural Philippines is very open and gossipy, and nothing would add grist to the rumour mill more than a scandal – not even a button loosed yet – between Mena and me. I met her coming out of Mass this morning. We said hello and passed on. The gospel was 'Greater love than this . . . ' and she knew that I was speaking to her, from some of the things in my sermon.

So there's Kennedy for you. Her hunger touched something very deep in me. I am unable to make a judgement about her or myself or celibacy or the priesthood. I'm just paralysed.

Much of my trite philosophising about Alice, ten thousand miles and fourteen months away, is gone up in smoke. I feel nothing has changed there, except some new layer has come down here and I'm not even interested in being decisive about it.

Those black, lonely nights here, Annette, do something to a man. She's brown, and totally different to me. The only thing we have in common is need. I don't know whether it's psychological or sexual, but it is desperate. We'll live with it until we can prudently get

213

away again, and when we do it's not going to be any less intense than before.

I have convinced her next year to do her thesis. I don't want to begin an affair with a woman who wants children and I don't. Yet I cannot see myself not being near her. Have you any insights for a man in a mess like that?

Jim

Candelaria, 3 July 1976

Dear Annette,

The skies are blue again; the waters have subsided. I got my first newspaper in three weeks today, but no mail as yet. Things are kind of back to normal. I've reached the conclusion that though Candelaria has much to offer, it is a son of a bitch in the rainy season. The leadenness of the last two months got to me. What I miss most are people like you and Seamus to talk to.

While I was in southern Zambales, there was intense communication among us Europeans. Here, I'm on my own. Intense communication or dialogue on issues, such as I had with Seamus, O'Brien, O'Dwyer and a few more, can be a substitute for the emotional needs. We carried one another over the bumps. We worked, met regularly and compared notes. Here, I don't meet with anyone, and compare with no one. That, I think, was the reason behind my suicidal *affaire de coeur*. I wrote to Seamus a few days ago and told him how your friendly logic took the skin off me over it, and how I'll have to start praying to my guardian angel again.

I got your piece on Edna O'Brien and the diary of Frank Lanbach. Ever since I read *The Country Girls* and *The Girl with Green Eyes*, I have been a fan of Edna. She wrote another, *A Pagan Place*, I think, half of which is a stream of consciousness about her own girlhood. It was brutally real, if I know anything about some sectors of Irish life. She has a fantastic ability to face and express the truth about her Clare past. When she goes contemporary, she loses her touch. Read all three and forget about *August Is a Wicked Month*.

I do not vibrate with Frank Lanbach's thoughts and reactions to the Maranaws. He was more a mystic than a missionary. It's a tough prospect for any priest down there. Having shot my friend Martin Dempsey in 1970, they tried to desecrate his grave last year but failed to break through the masonry. When Lanbach says, 'The Crucifixion portrays God forsaking the finest example of loyalty we can find. God was betraying his staunchest defender. That cross, alone, is horrible . . . ' he hit the bull's-eye about Christianity. That's what it's all about.

12 August

I feel a gnat having to put this date. Your pre-Spain letter arrived and sparked me off. Since early July, I let correspondence pile up. I was mentally fatigued and couldn't face writing to anyone out of a vacuum.

Any part of the last three months is a long story. My prima donna, Vising Benavidez (aged thirty-six) arrived in late July and we're already at work. She looks like Chiang Ching, the wife of Mao. She's not a bit afraid of me. She's my sounding board for anything I do, and a laughing partner in a lot we should not do.

You asked me if I told Alice about Mena. The answer is *no*. With Vising, I come clean with everything, and when I told her about Mena, she wavered between patting me on the back and calling me an unprintable Filipino word.

I'll let this off to you now, and promise to give you a full report shortly.

Love, Jim

18

Dear Annette,

Last Monday I ordered 'Down tools' and Vising and I went up the Zambales Mountains to the Acoje mining camp to do a picture story (slides) on chromite mining. We ended up swimming in a deep pool in the Acoje River, miles beyond the camp, and not a human being in sight. She enjoyed it immensely, especially when I saved her from drowning. I discovered she couldn't swim only when, like St Peter, she tried to walk on water to get across to me on the other side.

Then the tropical rain came pouring down and our dry clothes became sodden. On the way back up to the camp, she asked me to stop, and pointed to yellow orchids, which I had to dig out of rotten tree trunks for her in the rain. The VW's insides became a mess of yellow mud, orchids, ferns and crazy leaves she took a fancy to. Her white habit, which she insisted on wearing after the swim, became ochre, and I had to sneak her into the convent to avoid giving lengthy explanations, since we had gone with the intention of photographing chromite mining in progress.

She's the nearest thing to Seamus I've met here and I'm keeping my fingers crossed that she'll be let stay on.

217

Acoje, she told me, played a big part in her life, fifteen years before, when she was a high school teacher in Iba and also worked as a provincial stringer for the *Manila Chronicle*. She had graduated from the University of Santo Tomas in Manila with a BA in journalism.

In 1961, a mining plane with four passengers crashed four miles south of where we swam, near the Coto mine in the municipality of Masinloc, and it was located only when two survivors emerged from the jungle ten days later. The survivors were the American manager of the mine, Micky Shaner, and his personnel manager, a Filipino. The pilot and a security guard, both Filipino, died. After ten days of fruitless search for the wreckage, the main reporters from the Manila papers had returned to base. Vising was immediately tipped off about the survivors by a friend of her father, and was able to interview them before they were carted off to hospital. She contacted the *Manila Chronicle* by radio-telephone, and that paper got the scoop.

As a reward for being a good girl, she was offered a job as a reporter in the newspaper's office in Manila, which she took, and gave up teaching.

Roughly what we're at is the following. We want to reach out in an intelligent, ongoing way to the poor, who are 50 per cent of Candelaria's eight thousand Catholics. We want to make it quite clear that the menu of our apostolate is going to be a bit different to Con O'Connell's. We've started with the 'conversion' of a group of married couples through a one-year programme. Eventually they will be able to reach out to other, poorer, couples, on subjects like responsible parenthood, family planning and marriage guidance.

Women, especially the poor, have a difficult life here, bearing one child after another, living no life, seeing no future, passing on their deprivations to their daughters in a vicious circle. Some of our couples are quite good at reaching out now, and the credibility which nuns and priests lack has been captured by them.

We have a TB-eradication scheme under way with barefoot doctors. Kieran and Seamus encouraged me in that. Twelve and a half per cent of deaths here are because of TB. We get free medicine, but we do the sputum for positive bacilli with a microscope. We wheedle X-ray film from the rich hospitals of Manila to be processed in Candelaria Rural. We have sixty cases on treatment already. Medication is administered in the home.

We filled out application forms for funds to repair an irrigation dam destroyed by the May typhoon, and by a freak got twenty-five thousand pesos from a rehabilitation agency. About seventy farmers who depend on a water supply for the planting season are now working round the clock. We are able to provide the building materials and the skilled labour.

And good news for you, angel. As of now, I have enough to finish off Rosella's education and for the TB scheme during the coming year. A cousin of my mother in San Francisco died last year, and willed me three thousand dollars. The day I got the cheque, I was driving around on baldy tyres. If you want to transfer that ten pounds per month, I can think of no greater charity, temporarily, than to give it to Annette Rowland.

I'm looking for a husband for Mena and I think I found him today – a young tennis-playing doctor in a southern hospital. I'm cooking up a scheme to introduce them.

I hear little enough from Alice. Maybe she's cheating on me! If she needs a man's touch to keep her alive, I wouldn't mind. I'm no big deal for a few months every four years.

In theory, Candelaria parish is a production centre for audiovisuals geared to evangelisation and development. We're doing a sound-slide thing at the moment for a November meeting of OCIC in Manila. I'm calling it *Fat God, Thin God*, a theme asking who we are and what we're supposed to be doing on this planet. The most common household icons in Philippines are the crucifix (thin god) and a fat and flamboyant version of Buddha (fat god), usually given as a wedding present. It's open to all sorts of interpretations, but with music and a soundtrack, it should be fun and get people to talk about themselves. We have taken about five hundred slides, with a little budget provided by Kieran, who has a knack of raising funds for special projects.

We had a bad earthquake in the south of the country recently, right in the middle of one of our mission areas. No casualties among us. One guy did get pinned under a falling cupboard, and from what I know about him, it's no harm at all that he suffered a little. I anticipate a slower rhythm over the next few months, and I should be much more disposed towards behaving like a Christian while I'm writing to you. The last three months are a blur and it's all because of Vising. She's driving me hard, and I like it.

Candelaria, 29 September 1976

Dear Annette,

A few moments ago I finished my supper, thanked Tina, my cook, left the *sala* to the flies and mosquitoes of the night and went to my screened bedroom to live out another night with myself.

In a flash of intuition, I became conscious of utterly wasting my time. My life was just a body sitting on a wicker chair while the cicadas chirped on the *ipilipil* outside the window. Do you ever experience flashes like that? I write to you about Alice, Mena and Vising as if I were an unmarried bank clerk in Surbiton. I don't know how to handle it. Is there something wrong with me?

Whenever I've tried to reflect on the dichotomy between the weakness of man and his nobility, I'm inclined to believe there's truth in the story of the Fall after all. I sometimes think of myself as trying to get back to that stage of absolute self-mastery and absolute freedom, but there is something askew with my mechanisms and it remains a dream.

One feels insecure and alone. I am more afraid of being alone and cut off than of death. As a matter of fact, I wouldn't give two damns about death. Sometimes I think it would be a release. I wouldn't have to probe any longer, listen to voices, wonder what a heart needed, what a soul needed.

Sometimes all I wish I had in life was a woman who could be quiet with me, and a child I could tell fairy stories to. People drag me like a golliwog. The hungry and the sick can anger me and sadden me. They affect me (like the woman in

221

the London Underground did you) and I become a victim with nothing but inward, sterile tears to mark my back-trail and a day's work which can scarcely be written in any logbook.

As I drove south to Olongapo yesterday, I began to wish Vising would miraculously become pregnant so we'd be forced to build a shack four kilometres off the road in Cabangan, where her father has twenty hectares of scrub with cattle and a bit of an asbestos mine. Vising is plain and moody, but can ask the right questions. We work as a team now for retreats, and have developed a real understanding of one another.

Just to finish up on this theme, which seems to be taking up most of my letters recently, I'd like to mention Mena.

Mena, for me, is a kind of goddess. She doesn't know it, but I need her as that. I cannot risk shattering an illusion if I come close to her. Vising is ordinary, like myself. She is the quiet woman for whom I'll walk the market in Olongapo in search of apples (they don't grow in Philippines), and whose silences and laughter give me peace.

Mena should be a flamenco dancer with a bullfighter husband who would show her off to the crowds.

It's all so strange out here, Annette. I am not able to become Filipino so that I can bridge the culture gap and communicate better. Ireland is as far away as Mars. My family and Alice are there, but I am not the 'me' here that I am there. I cannot separate myself. I have to live totally here when I'm here, and totally there when I'm there. I try to explain this only to you and to nobody else. Seamus is quite different to me in all this. He seems to be able to live within himself wherever he is. My emotions and sensitivities go out to and are conditioned by wherever I am.

Love, Jim

Candelaria, 18 November 1976

Dear Annette,

This is going to be a saga. About a month ago, I tried to write it for you, but the drama hadn't reached the last act. I may even send you the pages I had written. I got your marathon letter three days ago, and I wondered why you should be apologising for not writing when I am the real culprit. I liked it when you said our confidences to one another are brotherly and sisterly. I hadn't quite thought of it like that, but it is true that you are the only one to whom I pour out my fortunes without embarrassment. And when I write, I want my letter to be complete, an accurate reflection of how I feel and act.

This saga is about Vising. You got the introduction in my last letter. Now for Acts II and III.

She's gone.

We reached a stage three weeks ago where we either got married or separated. We separated.

A year or two ago, perhaps in the latter stages of my vacation in Ireland, I knew I was sold to South-east Asia. Whatever was left in me would be given in sunshine among the coconut trees. It wasn't a decision; it just happened.

I missed Seamus, though, as a reliable sounding board, and found ideas and plans building up in my mind and no one to sound off to among the priests of northern Zambales.

I went to Iba every Sunday evening for dinner and a game of cards with the bishop and some of the priests of the area. I would raise issues, but no one, especially the bishop, would respond.

One Sunday evening, after a stressful week of self-questioning, I blew off steam at the dinner table, and still the bishop stayed mum. After I left, Donal O'Dea said to Harry, the bishop, 'You're a quare bloody man, Monsignor. Here's one of your priests with questions on his mind. He's looking for leadership and you sang dumb.'

'This is not the place, Donal.' Harry said. 'Had I got involved in his questions, he would have interpreted what I said as being the mind of the bishop.'

To this day I do not know what Harry meant by that. I assume he meant that if he offered opinions, I would have to follow them. It was sad that these guys questioned nothing.

Then Vising came to help me with the audiovisuals and family life. In appearance, she looked like a mixture of Chiang Ching and Eleanor Roosevelt. She was low-key, keenly perceptive and intelligent. She's totally without guile and has a sense of humour.

We got on famously. She was above petty restrictions of convents, and when the mood came, she could grasp a good moment in life and enjoy it with me. She asked probing questions and I talked and talked. We journeyed here and there on business and became more at home with one another. We just held hands for weeks, holding back on an issue that had to be addressed. Eventually we did.

The tension centred on the priesthood and the sisterhood. For her, there was no third way, just two options –

religious vows or marriage vows. She was too honourable and too proud to settle for half a loaf. She is a mixture of Spanish, Chinese and Malay. I see now that she was right. For one week, I teetered on the brink of a decision, and then fate popped up and took some decisions out of my hands.

After a tense and emotional scene one day between us, I assented to her wish to try to live only as friends and co-workers. By this time, we were doing retreats and seminars on call. We were quite good, because she intervened where I was weak and I backed her up when she needed strength. Our knowledge of one another was almost psychic. So that we could continue with the work, we decided on a hands-off policy.

She got sick, and knowing that it was not a sickness that could be solved by aspirin, I wrote her a letter to cheer her up. The one thing I remember about it now is that I repeated my dream about a shack on the mountain above Cabangan, and that our relationship could only take off if, by some miracle, she got pregnant, even though we had never 'had sex' as they say. That would be the irresistible force to topple me from my pedestal of vacillation.

Anyway, she bounced back, but the letter, which she guilelessly left in her drawer, was found by one of the sisters and carried to Ma Mère, the head of the Congregation in Manila.

I live and work now with that sister who took the letter to Manila without consulting Vising. I have more pity than anger for her over what she did. In spite of one steamy night in our relationship, we had reached a level of working together which she and the other sisters could not credit or understand.

On the night in question, we were returning from Olongapo around midnight, and the timber bridge in Masinloc was down for repairs, so we had to pull off the roadside until it opened again at 3 AM. The unplanned delay was, as the moral theology books would put it, 'a grave occasion of sin'. Passions rose, bodies merged. We tried to make love in the back seat of the VW, but failed.

We didn't know how in such a confined space.

Vising was handled with kid gloves by Ma Mère and her council. They deprecated the sneaky way a serious issue was raised. Then they sent her to the Retreat House in Baguio for a month to pray about it and sort herself out. When this was over, she was assigned to Cotobato in Mindanao, as far away as possible from Candelaria.

Before that appointment took effect, we had one last get-together out of necessity in Manila. It was the Asian meeting of Catholic communicators – radio, TV and audiovisuals. It lasted a week, and our work in rural sound slides emerged as the winner in all media categories because of its simplicity, adaptability, inexpensiveness and effectiveness as a springboard to dialogue with people. They even gave us six thousand pesos to develop our work.

So there we were, quite successful on the surface, but underneath shattered by the blanket celibacy law of the Church we have tried to serve.

The tragedy for me is that I was all teed up for productivity on many fronts, but the heart is gone out of me now. I'm just hunched up, waiting for some load to lift, for some light to come which will illumine the darkness that surrounds me.

I'll start to build my furniture factory after Christmas.

226

Rosella is now directing a play for PETA, the folk-theatre company of the Philippines, and will teach in Candelaria next year.

But I'm lost without Vising. If we decide on marriage, we have a place picked out in Mindanao. Her uncle is a doctor with a chain of pharmacies and had asked her before to manage them. But we're not going to rush.

Mena is fine. She visits regularly with some of her co-teachers.

Love, Jim

19

Today is 10 March 2002 and there was snow with gale-force winds yesterday. I have decided to break with tradition and not go near the garden until the end of April or early May. Seed-catalogue companies would have you out in mid-March if you were stupid enough. The delay will also give me time to finish this in five more chapters.

Herself reads the chapters as they come off my little Oki printer and she thinks the last one is the best.

'Why wouldn't it be?' I ask. 'And you centre stage.'

'It took you seventeen chapters to get to me, though.'

'That's because I had a lot of women and things to dispose of first. Now you can bask in the spotlight until the end. I'm unhappy with one element of that last chapter, though.'

'What's that?'

'It's all my side of the story, my version of events. It would be nice to see it from your side, too – from the very beginning.

My name is Vicenta Benavidez, formerly known in these pages as 'herself', and generally known as 'Vising'. Fate is a word I use an awful lot. Maybe it's because I'm a Filipina, and Filipinos are fatalistic.

It was fate that Jim Kennedy met Sister JP at St Paul de Chartres College, Herran, Manila, the biggest third-level institution run by the Sisters of St Paul, and she told him about me. It was fate that Ma Mère overruled the objections of her provincial council and sent me to Candelaria. It was fate that we fell in love so strongly that Jim, who saw too many sides to every coin, was able to get out of a life assignment he wanted to quit but couldn't, because part of him was brainwashed.

But fatalism is only a tool we use if it suits us, like the Filipino *bahala na*. Philippines is a matriarchal society – with some exceptions, of course, like my father, who called the shots in my family, whereas his mother, Juana, called the shots in a big way a generation before. Women's lib never took root in Philippines because a version of it is rooted in our culture, and it would only upset the apple-cart to take the new liberation seriously. Women have always held the money bags in the Philippines, decided where the children are going to be schooled and for how long, and how much is going to be spent on fertiliser for the paddy fields next planting season.

Jim was too nice, too amenable, especially to women. He let himself be dragged around. He had to be sorted out, and I was the one decreed by fate to do it. Alice could have done it, but didn't. She had the greatest hold on him. I'm not saying I took over like some matriarch calling the shots. I provided, I believe, a complement which freed and then energised him, and which he found later he couldn't do without.

We have never thought of ending the relationship. It still works.

I've read all the letters he wrote to Annette with equanimity, and she has been to visit us twice, once when Seamus and Evelyn were here. The 'steamy' side of his life in Philippines was harmless. It went with the search, and once we married, he was freed of the search. It was a load off his back.

He was a very alive, congenial man, floundering because he thought too much, had too much respect for people and had to be rescued for his own good. I could not give him an out, settling for a 'third way' like Alice and Thu Thuy did. If I could appropriate a bit of the Temptation-in-the-Desert dialogue to suit my own purposes, I would say, 'Not on love alone doth women live.' He needed help, and I had to be uncompromising.

I needed help too, actually, but that's for later.

I have learned to write like Jim. He writes in short, clipped sentences. He doesn't have to elucidate because he writes simply and clearly and doesn't sermonise. He doesn't think for the readers, but allows them to draw their own conclusions. I agree with this. It's very like what we began to do in Candelaria.

The religious underestimate the intelligence of people. For the last twenty-five years, I've been learning that, and I trust lay people rather than the Vatican to chart the future for us, as Christians.

When we started working together in Candelaria, I needed the excitement of it as much as he needed a companion to replace Seamus. I had studied theology at the Sister Formation Institute of the Philippines, worked on catechetical and family-life programmes in parishes, and still had time left at night to edit my religious congregation's magazine. Yet I felt I was only marking time. The diet was growing stale, and the glamour of being a nun was wearing off.

Out of the twenty-one of us who entered the convent together in May 1967, only one was without a lay profession.

Damiana was a nurse with a PhD. Gertrudis, Sonia, Yolanda, Maria, Flordeliza C., Magdalena, Lolita and Edita were all primary-school teachers. Flordeliza and myself were journalists. Severiana was a chemist, and Lorna and Rosemary were nurses. Estrellita was an accomplished singer, trained at St Paul College's Conservatory of Music, as was Agnes, a professional pianist. Veronica was an accountant, Enriquetta was a dressmaker and Norma, at eighteen, hadn't yet begun her college education.

Only four of that group have left and married. Two died. Jim had twenty-four in his ordination class of 1958. Eight have died. Six left the priesthood.

I have always believed that there has to be an apex to one's life, a great moment, and if it doesn't materialise it should be made materialise. When I was sent to Candelaria, I certainly didn't expect to find it there. Candelaria was a small town within a closed, Zambal society – the poorest and most unenterprising town in all Zambales. Iba, where my father worked, is just an hour's drive away.

In spite of reading the big pitch Jim made for me in his letter and project proposals about Candelaria, given to me by Ma Mère, I knew most of it would be drudgery. And I would be working with a foreigner for the first time in my life. When Ma Mère asked my opinion on whether I'd like to go there, I told her honestly that I'd rather work within the St Paul College community.

My family had little contact with foreigners, certainly in Nueva Ecija, where most of the nine of us were born. My earliest memory is one of being carried on a carabao cart up the mountains to escape the Japanese in 1944. They were the only foreigners I had come across. We used to have to bow to them.

They'd come to our house and say, 'Cook rice, cook rice', and would eat it before it was properly cooked.

By the time the family transferred to Iba, the capital town of Zambales (because my father became District Forester), there were three American bases there and the Columbans had arrived to staff the parishes, so there was no shortage of foreigners after that.

From day one, Jim 'as foreigner' never materialised for me. Both of us came from a Catholic tradition going back hundreds of years, both of us were journalists, and he spoke Filipino but, understandably, not as well as I spoke English. Both of us had lost a lot of religious scruples and could slip with ease between the secular and religious personas, because no one can be 100 per cent pure religious all the time. He was close to forty-two and I was thirty-seven, so why did we get so steamed up over a barrel of peanuts?

Two reasons I'm sure of. The culture of the Catholic religion and its laws about sexuality, particularly the celibacy one, were deeply ingrained in us and we had to wrestle almost to the death over them. The culture of the Philippines was alienating Jim, because he couldn't come to grips with it on his own.

I remember him telling me graphically how he felt after the Candelaria Midnight Mass of December 1975. Everyone wished him *'Maligayang Pasko'* (Happy Christmas) outside the church. Everyone was happy. Their absent family members were home from Manila and Olongapo. The beautiful scent of the *damo de noche* was strong in the air. Eventually, all left to celebrate the *Noche Buena* (Christmas Eve) in their homes, and he was left alone in the silence. He walked into the *convento* with his head down, up to his room with the unemptied ashtray, makeshift furniture and the pile of paperbacks.

That was no life for this man.

During our four months working together, I saw that life could be great, not stale. I saw that a love relationship with a man was a plus, not a minus, and I became more and more energised by it. I had to balance my guilt against these pluses, and guilt lost. Yet I had to go into exile, because it takes two to tango and himself wasn't ready to. I doubted then whether he ever would be, and I had to get on with the rest of my life.

No one has done surveys on the internal havoc these relationships cause. They are ignored in the Church because they are not supposed to happen. If we were more transparent and realistic, we would expose all the suffering that goes on worldwide, before nuns and priests, or nuns and laymen, or priests and laywomen walk away from it all with no happy memories of Mother Church.

I have supported Jim in exposing ourselves to some who will take pot-shots at us when *Fat God, Thin God* is published. I'm happy to do so, because we would have betrayed some of the finest impulses in ourselves had we refused.

I actually believe that we are making a contribution to Christianity, and the day is not far off when priests, whether male or female, will have the option to marry. It is very sad for me, especially in these times when our Church leaders are taking a justified hammering over their covering up of filthy acts of sex abuse by some of their priests, that Jim and I couldn't have continued our work in Candelaria as a couple, recognised and blessed by the Church.

When we participate in the acculturation talks with the newly arrived Filipino nurses, Jim is really able to communicate

233

with them. I think it's because he knows, particularly from his feelings of twenty-five years ago in the Zambal town of Candelaria, what culture shock is all about. You'd imagine I would be the one to get them on their toes – a fellow Filipina with twenty-five years of adjusting to Ireland. But I'm a bit like Seamus, able to live within myself. Jim feels more, and that's an asset in communication.

At this stage, Vising just said, 'I have enough written. Let you finish the story.'

Vising is a very private person and doesn't reveal herself very much – even to me. While we were discussing her input, I found out things for the first time. Like why she left the *Manila Chronicle* and became a nun.

Herself and her two sisters, Nene and Annie, lodged together while she worked on the paper. Nene was doing medicine in Far Eastern University, and Annie was studying social work in Philippine Women's University. The pace of life in Manila and the socialising jobs she had to do – attending fashion shows, hotel and restaurant openings, celebrity dinners and so on – for a Sunday-supplement woman's magazine left her feeling alienated after a year.

'I wasn't that kind of a socialite woman,' she said, and I can believe it.

She went back to Iba and resumed teaching, but this time in the Catholic high school run by the Sisters of St Paul de Chartres. Two of her students were Vicky and Mike, the two youngest of the Benavidez family. Dinny Egan, a Columban from Ferbane in Offaly, was the parish priest and became her confessor. She confided in him that she wanted to become a contemplative nun with the Pink Sisters in

Baguio. Dinny supported her and gave her a good recommendation, which she sent off with her letter of application. The reply suggested that she might not be cut out for the contemplative life.

'That's it,' Dinny said. 'You're cut out for the active life now. Join the Sisters of St Paul de Chartres.'

And she did.

Dinny is now retired in St Columban's, Navan, and we meet him once in a while. He is a kind and saintly man.

20

Candelaria, 8 February 1977

Dear Annette,

You have gone into hibernation and I aim to poke you out of your cave. I want to tell you two things: I'm thinking a lot about you, and I intend to spend a week with you, perhaps immediately after Easter.

Firstly, I couldn't cross the final bridge to Vising, although it was touch and go. I'm taking tranquillisers for the first time in my life, but in a month or two I'll be OK. She's all right.

I feel as if I've joined the Flat Earth Society, but there it is. I've left a trail of debris behind me. Alice feels injured and betrayed. That relationship is kaput too, for keeps. It must have been a man who conjured up the line 'All is fair in love and war', but it does no good for me.

My work has gone to hell – the active, mental side of it – although I still keep following the blueprints, but with the conviction of a sleepwalker. I am very glad to have someone to write to, although I want to forget about the whole thing. Truth may be one of the great virtues, but to discover it in an anguished, emotion-charged tropical aloneness is no joke.

Secondly, I'll robot on until March and then I'll go home and walk the fields of Brackile for a month. Then I'll come back and begin again. The truth for me is that this priesthood with which I've inflicted myself won't lie down and die unless confronted with a logic I don't possess, or a superior force not yet on the horizon.

If you are not bored with my juvenile delinquencies, I'd like to stay with you for a few days and I promise to be good company.

I now realise why Mike was attending a psychiatrist in Chile. Any man trying out the *adaptacion total* (Spanish for 'going native') in a strange culture is, at some stage or another, with or without a woman, going to get as high as a kite. I was at the apex of that four days ago on a round trip to Olongapo.

I came very close to deliberately swerving off the road at the zigzag near Olongapo and crashing hundreds of feet into the South China Sea. Despair is a terrible feeling when it's at its blackest. On the way back I called in to the *convento* in Iba to ask Donal O'Dea to come with me to Candelaria and to prevent me, passing through Masinloc, from sending a telegram to Vising saying, 'I'm ready. Let's go.'

He came with me and, of course, I didn't send the telegram. I wasn't even in a fit condition to drive (and it wasn't alcohol), not to mention make an irrevocable decision.

The highlight of my day's productivity now is to sit on the edge of my garden wall and watch the workers build our little furniture factory. We will go into production when I come back, hopefully, cured.

Candelaria, 17 March 1977

Dear Annette,

You seem to have gone underground. Haven't heard from you now since before Christmas. How the hell are you?

My last note said I might be passing your way around Easter. That plan has been scratched, and if I go at all it will be the end of August or September.

Am in good shape now, at peace with the world and myself. Like the confident Saul of Tarsus, I was struck off my horse and lost a few of my illusions. It has something to do with being forty-two, coming to the end of one existence and beginning another.

Vising proved a tremendous friend throughout the whole thing and what was an earthy relationship before, fluctuating between torture and ecstasy, has now become the deepest friendship I've ever had. All our little secrets, fears and inadequacies were exposed to one another during those three traumatic months. I discovered a great indecisiveness in myself on a real issue, and discovered too that it is only when the scent of death is in my nostrils that I can move, temporarily.

Deep down I know she will not go away, ever. It was the great moment and it will come back some day. For now we carry on because of this blasted celibacy law.

I heard from Seamus recently. Himself and Evelyn are going home slowly from the Yemen through Europe in July, and want to rendezvous with me in London or Ireland in August. Apparently he must be fairly sure of the fellowship in Fordham.

Rosella is graduating in the honour roll in a few weeks' time. She is coming to work in April and beginning it with a three-week drama workshop for the locals. I can see her drama and theatre supplementing the Vising-less audiovisual programme, if not actually substituting for it. Rosella has given me some very nice things in basketry which you are responsible for, and which I will send to you later on.

It's beginning to get very hot now and any surplus blubber I've put on in the last three months will come dripping off between now and June. Take up your pen and write, for God's sake. Even two lines to let me know you're OK would do.

Candelaria, 6 April 1977

Dearest Annette,

I'm overjoyed to hear from you. I know only too well myself how one can be dragged at the end of a rope for months on end and merely have ambition enough to escape from life, not stir it up. My last letter to you said I wasn't going home at Easter but in August or September. I will therefore see you on my way home in late August. Seamus and Evelyn will rendezvous with us too.

The reason I went on about this Easter thing was that I wanted to get out quickly to put the pieces of myself back together. There's no longer any need of that now.

I went to see Vising in the most southern city of the Philippines, General Santos in Cotobato.

Perhaps it was an impulse not to let go of the great moment that took me on the plane journey – first stop at

Davao and then a short hop to General Santos. As the plane was coming in to land at Davao, there was an engine on fire, which more amused than frightened me. Filipino pilots rarely lose planes.

I was put up by the Passionists and then went to visit her in the convent. We had two wonderful days together. The priests gave me the use of their jeep to tour around and see the countryside. The sister in charge of the convent knew our story, of course. (Even the dogs in the streets of Masinloc knew it, because the RCPI people couldn't keep their mouths shut about the contents of my telegrams to Vising and revealed them to one of the Columbans. I hope it brightened up their miserable lives in that kip of a town.)

We've resigned ourselves: marriage is out. We're just happy to be alive and sane, to be able to write often and hold hands once a year.

The eye of a typhoon passed over us in Manila in 1971. It was the eeriest feeling, to be in a raging storm one minute and in the calmest of calms the next. Within eleven minutes, the storm was back, raging as before, but only from the opposite direction. A ten-metre-high acacia tree in the lawn was blown down before the eye passed over, but was straightened up and tossed the other way after the restart by the force of the wind.

In Cotobato, Vising and I were in the eye of a typhoon. Long may it last.

I'm back at work and enjoying it – fully aware, though, that a vital half is missing.

In your letter, you certainly gave old Mother Church a few fine kicks in the knickers. I'm not as angry as I should

240

be. My mother's crowd are long-suffering. The Church I see here – the poor relation of the haughty Anglo-Saxon Church (there's no Irish Church; that died around 1200) and Latin Churches – is a more vulnerable, searching institution, against which I cannot maintain a lasting rancour. If there's something inhuman in it, they outflank that part with a little two-facedness – they say yes to it and no to it at the same time.

I'll give you an example. A Jesuit I met had done a survey in some southern Philippines diocese – I think it was Bohol. He found that 70 per cent of the priests were living either openly or secretly with women, and the bishop turned a blind eye. Yet when the Filipino bishops participated in some sort of consensus in Rome during Vatican II, they voted to retain celibacy. They'd lose episcopal face if they didn't, but could still turn a blind eye at home.

Did you read *Cancer Ward* yet, by Solzhenitsyn? You would like Vera and Kostoglotov.

This week is one of the big weeks in Philippines, *Mahal na Araw*, or Holy Week. I'm introducing live Stations of the Cross at intervals on a route around the town. Each of fourteen *puroks* (part of a barrio) will create a human tableau of each Station and the procession will stop and pray in front of them.

The turnout is so big and the feel for pageantry is so genuine that I'll have no problem with it. People would make a laugh of it in Ireland, even if you could get them to perform street-side. My Holy Week liturgies bear no resemblance to those in your place of worship. I do enjoy being a pastor and a bit of a prophet.

That hit me forcefully at the end of my period in the desert, and while I got grey hairs, which Vising was happy to see, she is glad I'm doing what I'm really best at.

I don't have as many strings to my bow as Seamus.

Regards to the three, and love, Jim

21

I'll have the substance of this finished within a month, leaving me plenty of time for affairs of the garden instead of affairs of the heart. My sister, Mary, whose judgement I trust, lives within two blocks of me. She is a good sounding board for each chapter as it is born. She thinks *Fat God, Thin God* is a good and unusual story, which is a boost to my ego. Vising and I are too close to it to make objective judgements. Nobody else, apart from our children, Patrick and Noriana, both adults, know anything about it. They sneak reads from pages lying around, and seem to be rather bemused that their parents once had a sex life.

Vising is working on a series of meditations fuelled by André Compte Sponville's *A Short Treatise on the Great Virtues* and the *Jerusalem Bible*, with one of our bonsai collection as a visual for each virtue.

She would have made a contemplative.

This is the dénouement chapter. The unexpected happened early in May of 1977, when Vising was elected a delegate to her congregation's provincial chapter to be held in Baguio, the cool mountain city in north-west Luzon. She came up from Cotobato, stayed with her parents in Iba for a day and got in touch with me. I volunteered to drive her to Baguio.

I can recollect that long journey along the coastline of Pangasinan and up the dangerous zigzag road to Baguio City with great clarity. We stopped in Damortis, a little railway siding en route, walked about, took photos of one another and generally behaved like children on a school outing. On reaching Baguio, it was much too early for her to go to the convent, so I kept on driving until we were ten miles north of the city and in breathtaking scenery.

She talked about herself and the support she was getting from all her Sisters, who knew what she was going through. She felt the intervention of God and spoke about it with wonder. Had she not been trusted and supported, especially by her top superiors, she and I would have found the excuse we were looking for. Sister Milagros Ycasas (who, as a member of the provincial council, voted against her being appointed to Candelaria) told her that by means of all this human agony and ecstasy, she would love me more and better, but in a way we were incapable of understanding then.

Well, the best-laid schemes of mice and men . . .

We had climbed up the side of a crag and spread a rug on the only level place we could find, a square metre of sand in a dried-up gully. A wide, deep valley lay beneath us, and the jagged peaks of the Benguet Mountains overlapped one another to a fifty-mile-distant horizon. The rice terraces of Banaue, Philippines' eighth wonder of the world, weren't too far up the road. We had talked and talked and the tension we had first felt in one another on meeting that morning was gone. We were at peace.

We needed one another desperately, and we did what lovers do on beds of sand in lonely ravines on high mountains since time began. The happiness during the whole trip was a prelude to it.

Dusk was falling as we were descending the bendy hairpin road to Baguio City. We had prayed together before we left, tears running down our faces. Black ants had been all over our clothes – those we had on and those we had off – but, blissfully locked in one another's arms, we hadn't noticed.

We had felt near to God. We wanted to give thanks, so we called into a contemplative convent of perpetual adoration and sat down for an hour, side by side. It was the Pink Sisters' convent – the same ones who thought Vising wouldn't make a contemplative.

The atmosphere, the mood in the little visitors' chapel outside the grill, dividing the cloister from the public area, affected me deeply. Benediction came on.

The singing was the way only nuns, experienced in it for centuries, can do it. About thirty of them knelt there, each at her prie-dieu, with their backs to us. They never bent, swayed or nodded. They had a freshly laundered look – not a pleat out of place in their buff-and-pink habits. When they filed out after Benediction, their genuflections were in perfect harmony, their hands joined in exactly the same way. They made no noise. The candles flickered and reflected on the golden monstrance.

I began to think of Ancient Rome and vestal virgins and the need civilisations seem to have for perfectly choreographed ritual. It was a glimpse of some other world which impressed me, affected me, but which I could never see myself belonging to.

I was thinking of Vising on the mountain – poor, plain, tortured Vising with her skirt up around her waist and the black ants crawling up her thigh. And while God was present among the freshly laundered, meticulous, worshipful ladies of the Pink Sisterhood, I only saw him and felt him on the mountain.

The tears, the tension, strands of Vising's cropped hair

matted in sweat, the wide-open fullness of love in her small body, the resolution and courage in her face showed me the God I knew. A God who asked that 'the chalice be lifted', while in a cold sweat of agony, a God who moaned that he was forsaken, looking down on freshly laundered Romans.

I delivered her to her convent and we said goodbye.

Back in Candelaria, I was calm. The calm had been given to me by her love and agony. Some sanity and purpose had been returned to me by her, who knew I had been throwing them to the winds in a mad scramble to live life part man, part God. I knew then I would always be like that. I wrote to Annette, telling her that if I ever changed, she should bury me.

One day, over a month later, I received a telegram from Vising in Manila. Her congregation's provincial chapter was over. She wanted to see me.

I went to the convent on Herran Street. Herself and Sister Milagros Ycasas greeted me and asked did I have a nice trip and so on.

Then Vising said, 'Your dream has come true.'

'Which one?'

'The one concerning the mountain above Cabangan, and repeated in the stolen letter.'

'Good God!' I exclaimed. 'A miracle!'

'A dénouement, certainly,' offered Milagros drily.

I drew myself up to my full five feet, eight and three-quarter inches, faced Milagros and asked her, 'As the representative of your congregation here present, may I, at long last, have the hand of Sister Vicenta Benavidez in marriage?'

'Highly irregular, of course. Ye are going to do it anyway, so, in the circumstances . . . '

246

'Will you marry me?' I asked, turning to Vising.

'Let me change out of this habit first,' she replied. And then the three of us laughed and laughed. The irresistible force had arrived, and so began the third part of our lives. I was glad it began with a laugh. Laughter had been missing from us for far too long.

I drove back to Zambales quite a different man to the one who drove down. There was a full stop and a capital letter between the two trips, so I began to think of the new paragraph, and only the new paragraph, not those after it.

I would visit Regalado and Vicenta (Vising was named after her) in Iba, and I would ask for the hand of their daughter. I would do it like a man and wouldn't wait for Vising to prepare them for it. She had to remain in Manila for a day, to sign exclaustration papers and officially leave the sisterhood. I was enthusiastic to get dug in immediately.

While that was a noble aspiration, it turned out to be an error of judgement. I didn't really know Filipina mamas, especially mamas who were very close to the Church.

I began by hesitantly putting our relationship in perspective and emphasising that while it was quite unusual for priests and nuns to get married, it was happening regularly in the post-Vatican II era. Rather than let them find out from Vising, I said, I thought I should take the responsibility on myself and ask for her hand in the time-honoured way

Vicenta took a dim view of my proposal. The Church and its trimmings were big in her life. She belonged to all the women's associations and was a daily Mass-goer. Regalado was phlegmatic. He waited for the storm to blow itself out and offered me a drink, which I didn't refuse.

Regalado, who was a member of the Knights of Columbanus in the parish – later becoming Chief Knight – could be as religious as a Filipino bishop. He could say yes and no at the one time to the same proposition and feel perfectly consistent.

'Ye are of age,' he said. 'Ye have decided on this. It is a decision which nobody but yourselves have a say in.'

Then he asked me the questions I had no answer to, yet. 'Where will ye live? How will you support my daughter?'

'I have no answer to those questions, but I will look after your daughter. It is a big relief to both of us to be able to leave religious life and live together. It was going to come sooner or later, and it has come now. I would be grateful if we could stay with you until we finalise our plans.'

'You are most welcome to stay with us while you are planning your future together,' he said.

When Vising came home and had a chat with her mother, whatever reservations Vicenta had vanished, and she became my biggest supporter and helper during the time I spent with them. I can still remember the way she tried to cook meat the European way, to please me.

When I got back to Candelaria, the room wasn't as grotty as it always looked on my returns. It was actually irrelevant, in the new scheme of things.

But I had other things to sort out. Rosella? I would release her from her promise to work with me in Candelaria. The furniture factory could become a home-economics room for the school. The TB scheme had funding for a while and it would be up to my successor to continue with it or not. The audiovisual programme would have to be discontinued. The biggest loser there would be Holy Mother Church.

The big truck, which I bought for a song from the US Navy

to haul the raw materials for the furniture from the mountains, would have to be sold. I had no personal money. Everything I had had been ploughed into the parish. Forward thinking? The Kennedys aren't famous for it. Read *The People Who Drank Water from the River!*

I wrote a long letter to J.W. with the 'bad news'. It's only when J.W. gets 'bad news' that he becomes a knight. Confronted with the daily routine of the priesthood, he is just ordinary. He went to my two sisters in Dublin and did a diplomatic job for me, in advance of me telling my mother by letter. Both shed tears.

The first paragraph was then complete.

22

It is difficult to imagine what it was like for me, after twenty years as a priest, to wake up one morning and find Jesus off my back.

I had responsibility for no one now but Vising and the small life growing within her. I had no responsibility to save the world, or anyone's soul but my own. It was such an incredible relief that it made me realise how seriously uptight I was about my mission in Philippines.

Some time during the nineties, the Columbans invited the former Columban priests to join the Columban ex-seminarians for a dinner. It was the first time the ex-priests were ever invited back to St Columban's, being pariahs, canonically. John O'Connell, the then Irish regional director, and Kieran Heneghan had something to do with this advance in thinking. The ex-seminarians were always considered legit – decent guys who had the wisdom to accept that they wouldn't be able to hack it in the big priestly world.

We, on the other hand, lacked that wisdom, and had to do an about-turn because of sex or politics or theology or drink or something – never because there was anything wrong with the Church.

A dozen or so of us, ex-Columbans, meet once or twice a year in a Dublin restaurant and we still have great fun, talking about the old days and the differences in our lives now as laymen. Joe2 is the group's catalyst and, depending on how much drink we've had, I believe the Church could learn a thing or two from our exchanges. I suggested a name for our association, the Judas Iscariot FC, because we had eleven 'players' and a substitute or two.

I was invited to say a few words at that dinner.

I suggested that the reason many of us left was that we hadn't enough real work to keep us occupied, and when I explained the relief I felt that Jesus was off my back, my classmate Owen Doyle, at another table, quipped back, 'Maybe he was glad to get off your back!'

Owen, still a Columban, and myself could slag like that because both of us had outgrown the strict definition of priesthood.

The Filipinos in Zambales would still call me 'Father' but I would no longer be part of the inner, clerical circle, or share in community goodies like health care. There would be no redundancy or pension scheme for years of service, and that has continued to this day. I would have no CV, because my existence as a Columban would be wiped clean. I would be an outsider, and I would have to learn to live with it.

It is only when the hiatus actually happens that the cold feeling begins. It cannot be anticipated. That cold feeling dissipated when Vising and myself took up temporary residence in Iba. It didn't go overnight, but it lessened day by day in the warmth of a germinating family life.

I was lucky, I suppose, because deep down I never saw priesthood as an exclusively clerical thing but as a prophetic thing, open to everyone who had the charisma.

We celebrated the rescue of one another as a big event, a positive and progressive step for us. There was no guilt, only sadness that the Church as an institution could not share our joy at becoming whole. That, we felt, would come in its own time, but we couldn't sensibly have waited around for it.

I explained to Vising and her parents that I didn't need permission from the Church to marry. I was free to marry, but, out of deference, I would hang on for a while, hoping for a quick laicisation.

Vising could have hers done in a day, but the Church made it difficult for me, a man. That in itself was incontrovertible proof of the sexism in the Church. Both of us had similar missions, were similar people, did similar jobs and had similar talents, yet one was treated less seriously than the other.

My bishop, Harry Byrne, knew about the dénouement before I went to see him to tell him he'd have to find a successor for me in Candelaria. When I told him I was leaving the priesthood too, he exhorted me to remain on, as 'the Lord had a lot of work for me to do yet in his vineyard'.

'What about Vising?' I asked.

He didn't answer. He just quoted John Donne and there was a drawn, grey look on his face, which I had never seen before. 'Doth the bell toll for me or for thee?'

Years later, when Harry was dying in a Manila hospital, his youngest Columban in my time, Declan Coyle, visited him and mended some fences that had been torn down while Declan was practising liberation theology in his diocese. Harry acknowledged a message from Tony O'Dwyer and myself, sent to him in a letter from Kieran Heneghan, offering our best wishes from Ireland.

'The tears rolled down Harry's face,' Declan said, after he, too, had nice things to say to him on his deathbed. Harry, as

Harry, a nice man, had nothing to apologise for, but Harry, as bishop, felt he had let us down.

He hadn't really. The Vatican, which closed its eyes to the signs of the times, and which he obeyed without question, did.

Declan left the priesthood and got married in the early nineties. He lives in Dublin with his wife and two children, and is a member of the Judas Iscariot FC.

After my meeting with Harry, I decided to go to Manila to cash in my chips with Peter Steen, the Columban regional superior in Philippines. He didn't put up any argument and, being a nice guy – something for which the Columbans are famous – just twisted his swivel chair round and, reaching for a filing-cabinet drawer, said, 'I must have the forms to be filled up here somewhere.'

Both Columban Steens, Peter and Paddy, played a coincidental role in my being a Columban. Paddy presided over my arrival in Dalgan Park for the first time in August 1952. Peter saw me out.

'By the way,' Peter said, a little bit embarrassed, 'You'll have to see a psychiatrist as part of the requirement for leaving.'

'Is that to see if I'm mad or if I'm sane?' I asked. 'Which?'

'It's red tape.'

I met the psychiatrist. It was all blah-blah to satisfy someone in Rome.

Back in Iba with Vising, both of us decided that we would use a few weeks of our time just enjoying ourselves, having a little vacation. We had suffered a lot of nervous exhaustion. It was a nice atmosphere. Vicenta and Regalado couldn't have been more helpful. Regalado's garden of orchids and fruit trees and his rice paddy beside the house made a lovely background.

I had time to think back to things which were only a blur when I was going through them. Whereas I was a spectator to Tony O'Dwyer's troubled going, to Connolly's sideways route out, and Brian William's dramatic exit, I was now in the middle of the drama myself.

I had witnessed Brian Williams leave Subic and I was mystified and saddened at the suddenness of it. I wondered if the guys were equally mystified by me. I didn't see Brian's exit as 'breaking ranks'. He was a bright, handsome young priest, and his next big day would be walking up the aisle with his Filipina bride.

Donal O'Dea and Colm McKeating knew I had been wrestling with the thought of marrying for months. Brian told nobody of his intentions.

It could have been the day I had the suicidal impulse on the zigzag coming into Olongapo from the north that I met Colm, a Belfastman, on the streets of Olongapo. I told him I was at my wits' end. He parked his jeep on the street, jumped into my car and said, 'Let's go to Manila. Right away. We'll talk on the way down.'

I can't remember anything of what was said, but I thought it was quite magnanimous that he would act without thought of whatever business he had in hand. His jeep could have been stolen, for starters. Jack Hynes and Lulu, his new wife, came to Candelaria also, while Vising was in Cotobato. Seeing that he had been able to make a decision to marry, I asked him to walk the beach in Libertador with me in the hope that, man to man, he could help me.

'No one can tell you what to do, Jim,' he said eventually. 'It's too personal a decision.'

During that period in Iba, I remember a few more personal

254

acts of great kindness by Columbans. Kieran broke ranks and invited both of us for dinner to St Joseph's, Olongapo. So did Donal Bennett in Castillejos, and in the way only Donal could throw a party. Vising said it was sublime. Kieran gave Vising an engagement ring with two pearls. Fintan Murtagh took us for dinner in the US communications base in San Miguel. O'Dea dropped in to see us in Iba, and we spent a day in Shay Cullen's place, packing things in a box to be sent on to Ireland. Donal McDonald got in touch with his brother Dermot, then Master of Holles Street National Maternity Hospital, to look after Vising. And Tom O'Grady took the two of us to the British Club, me for the second time, Vising for the first.

I often talked to Regalado about his *rancho* in the mountains and eventually made him take me there. It was upland, *cogon*-grass country, which would offer poor fodder in the dry season, but it did have a stream. His fifty cattle were there, as well as two Aetas whom Regalado chose as caretakers and who were doing a good job. He seemed regretful that none of his four boys was interested in it. They had gone into commerce and various types of engineering.

I saw possibilities of developing the place and asked Regalado many questions about it.

'A priest becoming a farmer?' he joked.

'My father made his money out of cows. I know something about cows.'

'What would you do?' he asked.

'I'd open a road into it first. The truck now parked outside your house, awaiting a driver to transport chromite to the docks in Balogannon, would be vital for that. It has an automated pulley and steel hawser up front. Once the place is accessible,

I'd stay up there five days a week in a nipa hut and plant *ipilipil*, which as you know grows up to three metres high per year. Posadas told me their leaves are very nutritious for cattle. Vising can go back to teaching again.'

'Cattle don't have long necks, and can only reach upwards to the height of two metres. What will you do then, when your trees reach a height of four metres? Exchange the cows for giraffes?'

'I'll cut the *ipilipil* down and make fodder nuts from the leaves, like the grass-meal nuts we have in Ireland.'

'Do you know of a machine to make them?'

'No, but I'll go home to Ireland and find out all about the process. All we'll need is steam and compression. We don't need a drier. The sun will do it.'

Both of us got enthusiastic.

I had been thinking of visiting Ireland to see my family. I used to wake up at night thinking of the gap I had created, and on one such night I said to Vising, 'I have to go home for at least a month, but we will get married civilly in Manila before I go.'

We went off to Manila for a few days and had the banns posted in the municipality of Makati, where Vising's sister, Nene, and her husband, Alex, both doctors, held positions.

We stayed in a hotel, a kind of advance honeymoon. I still had some of Tom Breen's dollars. We bought wedding rings and even had a wedding photo taken, ahead of the event.

The banns needed nine days of posting, and on the sixth day, when we were due to return to Zambales, Vising had a bright idea. 'I'll ask Alex to ask the mayor if he can speed up the process so that we won't have to come back down from Iba again.'

We were lucky. Mayor Nemesio Yabut would marry us in two hours. Alex and Nene wouldn't act as witnesses, because of some Filipino or family pisheogs, but would get two people from their office to deputise.

Yabut, who died of a heart attack in 1986, was the most important mayor in the country, reigning over the richest part of Manila. His office, with only one big desk at the farthest end from the entrance, was huge. We were paraded in and took our seats in front of him.

'Ah, James Kennedy, an American,' he said, looking at the names on the prepared marriage certificates.

'Irish, actually,' I said.

'And what is an Irish doing in Zambales?'

I'm with a multinational company,' I explained.

'Doing what?'

'Development.'

'Of what?'

'Farming, health, education and so on.'

'Like one of those UNESCO things?'

'Exactly.'

'Filipinas make good wives and mothers,' he told me. 'Many of their marriages to Americans go wrong. How are you sure yours won't go wrong?'

I thought this question very funny in the circumstances, and had to bite my tongue before answering, because during my time in Subic, I had performed many Filipino–American weddings, but had refused even more. I considered myself an expert forecaster of connubial bliss or misery between Filipinas and Americans, and acted on that instinct.

'Because we have many affinities,' I carefully replied.

'Such as?'

'Psychological . . . spiritual . . . '

'Yes, go on.'

'And biological.'

'Tell me about the biological.'

'I plead the Fifth Amendment on that, because it would not be in the lady's best interests here, *sa harap ng karamihan* (in front of people).'

He had a laugh at that. 'You speak Filipino. Good. Few Americans honour us so.'

The dialogue lasted for twenty-five minutes. This is all I remember of it on that day, the seventh of the seventh, '77.

He asked Vising one question, 'Are you happy with this man?

About to become the dutiful wife, she answered, 'Yes.'

Then, with a flourish, he signed the certificate, told us and the witnesses to do likewise, said congratulations and left after handshakes all round. Alex told us later that Mayor Yabut had never in his life taken twenty-five minutes to do a marriage.

Vising and I invited our witnesses, Adriano Sebastian and Leticia Gepilano, whom we had never met before or since, to our wedding reception in a restaurant. The bill for the four of us came to seventy pesos, about five pounds.

Vising recalled later that Mayor Yabut hadn't asked us to say 'I do' or 'I will.'

'Are we married at all?' she asked, with a worried look.

'It was the best marriage ceremony I ever attended,' I replied. 'And remember, I am an expert on that kind of stuff.'

Two years later, after Vising and Kieran kept nagging me, I agreed to go through a Catholic marriage ceremony, but only on condition that it was done in our own sitting room. How

Kieran wangled that concession out of the Archdiocese of Dublin I don't know, but it was done.

Like a Filipino bishop, I had learned to say yes to two opposing propositions and to feel perfectly consistent.

23

Balili, Iba, 26 June 1977

Dear Annette,

Your telegram and letter were real supports because I was in hospital in Manila with flu and gastroenteritis. Vising was with me every day. Right now she is stretched out beside me on our double bed, examining the signs of forthcoming motherhood. We are in Iba, where we have a room in her parents' house. If it's God's plan that we stay in Zambales, we'll add on a kitchen–living room and a bedroom for ourselves.

While we were in Manila, my sisters in Dublin telephoned me after receiving my letter, and they were wonderful. There are no international telephones in Zambales yet.

While I'm still experiencing the withdrawal pains from the snug life and am a bit anxious about the future, there is a remarkable peace in me. Zambales is one of the most beautiful places in the world, life is informal as well as full of possibilities, so why should we run away?

I leave for Ireland on Monday 11 July to see the family, scout out job prospects and study the technology of making a certain kind of cattle fodder. I'm keeping all my options open. I hope to see you on my way back

very happy. Impending motherhood is doing a lot for her. Her first month in Ireland will be critical, but I'm confident she'll not only make it, but enrich the family in the process.

I spent a while with a young Australian Columban, Colin McClean, who lives and works with squatters in Manila. His existence is hand-to-mouth, so I turned over your covenant to him. He's a great fellow. Then I met another ex-Columban, Neil Frazer, also an Australian, who married a Filipina a few years ago and lives among the Muslims in Mindanao.

What a man. I don't have one-tenth of his courage. He's doing community work with a Protestant group, specialising in photography and audiovisuals. He's only thirty-three and had made a movie in Australia while he was a Columban. I had the strongest feeling that he was the most all-round missionary I ever met. For months early this year, his wife, kids and himself were hungry. I gave him my photographic equipment. He has produced very touching stuff.

I was very well received here in our Central House. There is a discontent among some of the men, the symptoms of which I recognise from my own confusions. I spent one day listening to the intimate story of one chap in his late thirties, and it was almost a carbon copy of my own. As a result, he went back to the girl, is going home to prepare a nest and will bring her with him to Ireland too.

I don't believe these cross-cultural marriages are to be recommended to any Joe Soap (they are challenging and exciting but demand fantastic understanding and patience), but the likes of us walk into them because of our abnormal personal histories. One thing, though, can save us. Most of us have been in Sheol – hell – and there's only one direction to move in after that – upwards.

When we have a place of our own in Dublin, you will come over and be our honoured guest. Besides you and Seamus, we have but a few friends, and you will always remain close to us because of the style in which you shaped and supported Vising and me.

God bless, Jim

Donnybrook, Dublin
December 1977

Dear Annette,

The streetwalking has finished. By a stroke of luck, I fell in for a job as editor of four monthly trade magazines. I do an average of four articles for each – mainly company and personal profiles, which means I am on the road a lot, interviewing people. I'm enjoying it because I am a student of people. What I write is not always what the boss wants, but at least the bloody thing is readable.

We have put a down payment on a second-hand Renault 12L and *on a house*. My salary of five thousand pounds a year was enough to get a mortgage. The house is in Lucan, where my sister, Mary, lives with her husband and kids. We'll move there after the baby is born in mid-January. Vising is thrilled about it and her new life.

I just feel relief that my twenty-five-year odyssey is over and I'm back to where I started – a little wiser and a little greyer.

Love, Jim and Vising

24

My family never admitted it to me, but I know there was disappointment at my leaving the priesthood. No one feels disappointed now, but it was my mother in Brackile, going on eighty years of age then, who took the great initiative in leadership and brought all the family together in Dublin to meet Vising for the first time, a few weeks after we arrived in Ireland. It was a grand gesture from a noble lady, and in our relationships with them we have never looked back since.

On 23 October 1977, I got off the bus at McBirney's (now sadly defunct) to walk to my first job in Lower Mount Street. (At that time, Vising and I were staying temporarily with my sister and her husband in Lucan.) I was in tie and suit, courtesy of the St Vincent de Paul Society. Walking up Westmoreland Street towards Trinity College, my eyes were focused on the pavement ahead, on scores of feet coming against me. Clip-clop, clippety-clop. Mine, with scores of others going in the opposite direction, enacted a sort of early-morning street ballet I had never been part of before. All of a sudden I got an intense feeling of joy, of sureness from the motion of my legs and feet with all the others. It made me feel that I was back in the human race again – after twenty-six long years. In fifteen minutes, I would start working as an editor of monthly trade magazines dealing with transport, construction and the grocery trade – subjects I knew little about. At that moment, I didn't care. I felt I could do anything.

The new job, at five thousand pounds a year, gave us the credit to get a mortgage and a house in Lucan. Our adjustment processes were going on unobtrusively in the main, but sometimes obtrusively. Driving a nail into the wall of our new house to hang a picture, the staggering thought occurred to me that this was the first wall I had ever owned, and I a forty-four-year-old already. A can of 7 Up stood on a chair, and again it made me happy that I had actually bought it myself, from my own pay packet. I had always felt that the spending money I got as a priest was a kind of handout. One early morning, I heard Vising screaming at me from the bedroom window to get up and look. She was witnessing her first ever fall of snow. She stood in her dressing gown on the lawn up to her ankles in it, while I, embarrassed, photographed her as people passed by in their cars on the way to work.

A month later I took her to see Dalgan Park and met Barney Smith in the driveway. Barney and I had worked, dined and played golf together during the years I had spent on *The Far East*. Now Vicar General of the Society, he was his usual charming self, and asked Vising how she liked Ireland.

'It's grand,' she said, 'only for the fucking weather.'

The poor girl had no idea what the adjective meant, but had heard everyone using it. I blushed to the roots.

The Chancellery
Archbishop's House
Dublin 8
8 June 1978

Dear Mr Kennedy,
The Reverend Cyril Murphy, St Columban's, Navan, has asked me to execute the rescript of laicisation granted in your favour on 21 April 1978.

I would therefore ask you to sign the enclosed form and return it to me as soon as possible.

With kindest regards and wishing you every blessing for the future.

Yours very sincerely,
+Dermot O'Mahony
Auxiliary Bishop of Dublin

Conditions to be observed by the dispensed priest:

(a) He may not participate in the function of Sacred Orders except those enumerated in Canons 882 and 892, p. 2;

(b) He may not participate in any liturgical acts celebrated with the people where his condition is known, nor may he preach;

(c) He may not participate in any pastoral office;

(d) He may not act as rector or in any administrative capacity, nor as a spiritual director or teach in seminaries or similar theological institutions;

(e) He may not act as director of Catholic schools, nor

teach religion in any schools, Catholic or otherwise. This latter restriction is subject to change by the Ordinary of the place upon request of the dispensed priest;

(f) As a rule, the dispensed priest, and especially a dispensed priest who is married, ought to remain away from places where the fact of his ordination is known.

Lucan, County Dublin

16 June 1978

Dear Bishop,

Thanks for your best wishes and for expediting the rescript.

There is no reason why I shouldn't abide by paragraph (a) of the conditions you enclosed but I have no wish to compromise my chances of living an active Christian or professional life by agreeing to the others. The implications of some of them are a source of grim amusement to a forty-four-year-old trying to start life again in the competitive job environment and the threadbare socio-religious climate of Ireland today.

I hope this does not inconvenience the finalising of the papers but I would have been less than honest had I signed on the dotted line just to get it over with.

Very sincerely yours,

James Kennedy

The once-famous Society on the front lines of evangelisation for at least eighty years, the Maynooth Mission to China, or Columban Fathers, is now fading out. It tries to keep up with the world, but keeps falling behind, an old athlete in modern and faster-moving games.

When I browse through the Columban Society Directory to check what old friend is where and doing what, I notice that we, former Columbans, like Joe O'Grady, Tony O'Dwyer, Barry O'Hagan, George Gear, Hilary Shannon, Donal MacDonald, Seamus Connolly, Frank Keogh, Luke Waldron, Jack Hynes, Vincent Healy, Jack Houlahan, John Lynch, Brian Smith, Martin Crohan, Tony Roche, Pat Brady, Kieran Kenny, the late John O'Connell, Pat Healy and Tom Caffrey, *et alii aliorum*, have been erased from its contents. It's as if we never existed.

We, in contrast, feel we do not have to erase anything.

I visit Dalgan Park for the funerals of old friends, as do some of the above-named, who live in the Dublin area. We, the ex-priests, have a good rapport with one another and with the men we meet there, with whom we once shared life on the missions. I cannot explain to myself what happened long ago that keeps us still bonded, even though we have become toughened businessmen with wives and families and they walk the polished corridors alone with their thoughts, their breviaries and their rosaries.

Even though the institutional Church is condescending towards ex-priests, they are not. Their welcome is genuine. But there's a sense that an equanimity is missing among many of them, that hope has to be constantly worked on.

I am unequivocally glad I don't have to work on it, or on faith either. The latter comes and goes on its own, as it always did.

When I have to declare my religion, as on a census form, I still write 'Catholic'. Unrepentant as the Church is to the views of men and women like me, I still find my old religion the most comfortable fit – but much like a decrepit pair of old shoes one might miss if one threw them in the bin.

We could have invested a lot of ourselves in Regalado's *rancho* had things gone the way we wanted in 1977. Their going wrong proved a blessing in 1991 when Pinatubo, towering over the *rancho*, blew its top and covered the land feet deep in volcanic ash.

Epilogue

What I've written is about me – a humanoid – living, moving and thinking within a framework of tribe, religion and culture, much as other humanoids do on this planet.

We're born into races and places and religions and economies over which we've no control at the beginning. But one day, out of necessity or curiosity, we might move on, into a new tribe, a new way of looking at things, and we have to decide how much of our old culture we will hold on to and how much of our new tribe's culture we will absorb and be changed by.

We might even move again and again into new tribes and new cultures, discarding old attitudes and values along the way and taking on new ones. This sifting through our stored experiences is necessary to increase our self-knowledge, and ultimately, while this search for happiness is going on – that's what the sifting is really all about – we put some sort of final shape on our identities before we die.

That self-knowledge is about as much happiness as we are likely to achieve on earth.

The life story of any priest in the Catholic Church is boring. His is a structured, conventional life, with little melodrama. But had I become a plumber at twenty-four instead of a priest, my life story would still be boring. And it would also be boring if I had become a policeman, a lawyer or a shoe salesman. This makes us all boring people – if we only think of the mechanics of what we do for a living. But if, while we scrounge and serve and relate from day to day, we see ourselves as part of a wider process of civilisation involving global movement in thought and attitudes, then we are leaving ourselves open to the experience of intermittent interior change and may very well think of giving up the plumbing job to become a boatman on the Nile.

While having done nothing extraordinary within any of them at the time, I consider myself fortunate to have moved through tribes and cultures which were vastly different from one another.

My first culture was an ethnic one – a fairly typical rural, tribal Irish one. The second was ideological, the priestly culture in which I role-played a sanitised version of my real self in order to become some sort of universal model of humanoid which the Church wanted me to be. During part of that stage, I tried to integrate into the ethnic South-east-Asian culture of the Philippines, which was as different from my own Irish one as chalk and cheese.

The third, and the most difficult to adapt to, was the soulless, relentless culture of big business in which I had to dredge up the best remnants of my first two cultures in order to survive. I stayed in it because at the time I was too old and too afraid to risk moving on, no one offered me a job that suited me, and I needed the money.

I have one more culture to experience to the full: retirement. It is the culture of idleness and freedom and I have already embraced it like no other humanoid for one particular reason: it is the first time ever that I am free of the dominance of and away from the control of a sequence of masters whose common denominator was their belief in their own omniscience. Omniscience has been far from my mind in the last thirty years, and still is. I can only tell myself what to think and do – and no one else.

This came across most clearly to me during those seven years I spent in Philippines. I had a role there as the spiritual leader of two municipalities of Asian people, whose attitudes and values I was trying to understand in order to be able to lead them. Had I been able to acquire that cultural knowledge of them, I would have had a further problem: I wouldn't have known where to lead them, because the Church's authorities and its theologians were at odds with one another (and still are) over what evangelisation is really all about.

While I was wrestling with those problems, I was a culturally split humanoid – part rustic-but-educated Irish and part ersatz Roman. So I hadn't a leg to stand on, really.

But that didn't bother me. As my ancestors did on the hill behind the house in Brackile, I began to work it out for myself. Home from Asia, and not sure who the hell I was, I wrote the essays which became *The People Who Drank Water from the River*. It was an exercise in identity recovery. There is an ember deep down in the ashes of all of us, linked to atavism, which endures all cultural change and which can be relied upon in a crisis to get the fire going again.

Vising played a key part in getting the fire going again. With her I could maintain a live interest in the Philippines and its culture, a subject that still fascinates me. I learned much, but never enough. In hindsight, the biggest stumbling block for me during those Philippine years was that Filipinos don't feel they have to analyse themselves and reveal themselves as Westerners do. So I was talking to myself most of the time.

I am a compulsive poker into things. I see life as an evolution sequence, a tribe-growth sequence, a mind-growth sequence. I feel linked to the onward movement of history, and I have a part to play in it. If I thought I didn't have, I'd go to the elephant cave and die.

The sequences are vital. If I don't know what went on before me, I have no reference point to understand myself now. I am a link in the chain. If I don't make myself clear – especially today, when things are going as fast as lightning – how will my children, Patrick and Noriana, for example, know how the sequences connected with me and my era came about?

I remember my father not as a young, black-haired, even-tempered, entertaining husbander of land and animals but as a white-haired, often anxious, often cranky and occasionally entertaining old man in his sixties. I am like that now. When I die, my children will remember me like that.

In *Fat God, Thin God* I have given them another picture of an earlier sequence, when I had black hair, and thought all the thoughts I could and felt all the feelings I could and went on all the journeys I could, in an incredibly different world.

APPENDIX

A PERSONAL VIEW OF THE HISTORY
AND CULTURE OF THE PHILIPPINES

Among the nations of the modern world, the Republic of the Philippines is a geographical, cultural and political miracle. With almost 80 million people, seven thousand islands, up to thirty ethnic groups, a population which includes the world's richest and the world's poorest people, all speaking a combination of ten major languages and a host of minor ones, it has remained under the one flag and without major social upheaval of its own making in living memory. And this has been achieved as a democracy for almost sixty years – sometimes a faltering and uncertain democracy, but a democracy. Along with Thailand and Malaysia, Philippines has avoided the absolutist, authoritarian political solutions of its other neighbours – Vietnam, Cambodia, Laos, Burma, China and Indonesia – and since World War Two has lived in peace.

I regret now to say that all I noticed about it during my first few years there in the early seventies was its tantrums.

Congressman Crisologo was shot dead in 1970 as he came down from the altar-rails at Mass. Student radicals in the red headbands of Mao's Red Guards threw rocks at me in Quezon Boulevard in the capital, and one little squirt who (uncharacteristically for a Filipino) looked angrily at me, spat: 'Imperialista, go home!'

Not being the American he thought I was, I just accepted the insult and kept walking. I was only six months in the country then, but I had learned enough not to argue with a mob about my nationality.

Typhoon Yoling came in 1972 and flooded the riceland provinces between Pangasinan and Manila Bay, leaving millions hungry. I went two days without food at the time and was utterly flummoxed by the idea of it. For the first time, I saw galvanised sheets being ripped off roofs by the force of the wind and sail away like confetti in a breeze. My watch was snatched off my wrist in Singalong Street in Manila, outside the centre house of the Columbans, by a young man who I hoped robbed me more out of hunger than malice.

US Navy planes were flying in and out of Subic Base (two hours' drive northward from Manila) like bees around a hive. They were at war in Vietnam, eight hundred miles to the west. The same war brought US sailors with hard-ons ashore, on leave, to Subic Bay in their thousands and made the pimps and madams of Olongapo rich.

The English-language newspapers (using American spelling and news-speak) were full of 'slayings'. President Marcos was gearing himself up to reduce the levels of gun-smoke by declaring martial law – which was also to keep him in power until he was embarrassingly ousted in 1986.

All newspaper stuff. Political and social tantrums generally are.

But in the background, scattered throughout the islands, millions of Filipinos were going about their daily chores, ploughing and sowing, buying and selling, fishing and mending their nets, separated from all this, and not caring much about it anyway. Much as they had done in Spanish times.

Within two hundred years of the arrival of the Spaniards in 1521, the archipelago of the Philippines had changed irrevocably and dramatically. It was then – in the sixteenth and seventeenth centuries – that the modern Filipino emerged from the Luzon, Visayan and Mindanao tribes, and Spanish and Chinese *mestizos*.

Why the archipelago awaited the Spaniards for centuries, unmolested, is difficult to understand when some of its neighbours – kingdoms of the East like Siam, China, Arabia and Java – were at peak periods, their empires gobbling up territories all round them. Similarly it is strange that the great religions of the east – Hinduism, Buddhism, Taoism, Shintoism and Islam (which, with a head start of two hundred years, brought the Koran only as far as Sulu and the southern coast of Mindanao) – bypassed Philippines. 'Mother Asia,' as is often quoted on the islands, 'refused to share her soul with us.'

And so a ripe plum was left to Spain for the picking.

A case can be made that the islands – all seven thousand of them, allegedly, but only a dozen dominating the map – were an invader's nightmare. Geographically, they are in the earthquake and typhoon belts. The different tribes were no pushovers at defending themselves, as Magellan found out. He was killed in a fracas with natives shortly after reaching Cebu in 1521. A Chinese viceroy, before Magellan, is on record as dismissing the islands as a place 'only fit for snakes and savages'. There are seventy or more languages (often called dialects) in the Philippines. Nine of these are major languages, spoken by 80 per cent of the people. Ninety-five per cent of the people speak three languages: Filipino (Tagalog), the national language; the 'dialect' which is the tribal or provincial language; and English, which replaced Spanish as a second and compulsory language in school. The sheer number of major languages and tribes made it a logistical nightmare for any conqueror less faint-hearted, less focussed and less experienced than the Spaniards, who had the conquest of the Americas behind them.

When it came to the Christian evangelisation of the Philippines – which was as big a motive for conquest, under Philip II, as the economic one – the Spaniards were lucky. It wasn't as difficult as it could have been. Within fifty years of the arrival of Legaspi in 1565 (this was when the serious business of colonising began), a great majority of people along the coasts and on the plains had been converted to Catholicism.

This didn't make the Spanish friars the whizz-kid missionaries of all time, but it does draw our attention to two important factors they had going for them. For the pre-colonial Filipino, the new Christian religion didn't differ that much from his animist religion. There was a supreme God common to both, and while the new religion had a galaxy of saints as intercessors, the Filipinos had their own *diwatas* and *anitos* who acted as *tagapamagitan* with their god, Bathala. The belief system of the islands, therefore, with adjustments here and new emphases there, slipped easily into a Christian format.

The friars, unlike the more hidebound missionary of my time, had a genius for using and transforming the raw material they found. Because of this, a folk Catholicism evolved which I discovered was permeated by the miraculous and the supernatural, was heavy on ritual and celebration, was more about placating the spirits than transforming the world, and was occasional in worship, which, when it did happen, was enthusiastic, imaginative and involved the whole community.

The first Spanish friars were Augustinians who came with Legaspi in 1565. They were followed by the Franciscans (1577), the Jesuits (1581), the Dominicans (1581) and the Recollects (1606). It was the input of these men, particularly in their first two hundred years in Philippines, that determined not only the kind of Church I found when I got to the parish of Subic in 1971, but also much of the economic and political life I encountered there.

While Spanish government officials of that early period were content to live in the comfort of Intramuros, the old walled city of Manila, waiting for galleons to come from Acapulco, the friars departed to the outlying areas, establishing parishes and building churches. They had come to stay and later on most would row in with the Creole (a Philippine-born Spaniard) in his antagonism to Spanish-born, central officialdom as transient and symbolic of foreign authority.

But establishing parishes and building churches had a much broader meaning then than we realise today, simply because the Spanish friars were subject to far less mind control than us in their upbringing and could execute their job without looking over their shoulders at the moral policemen who monitored orthodox performance in the Church of my time. Nick Joaquin, in his book *Culture and History* sums up their contribution like this:

The friar planted crop after crop with no thought about how this might be to the benefit or detriment of the other mother country on the other side of the world. He was not thinking of the mother country, he was thinking of 'this republic', as he loved to call the Philippines. *'Esta corte'* and *'Esta republica'* resound repeatedly from his pages. He was – consciously or not – creating the idea of an independent realm. And everything he did increased that independence. Those crops he planted created economic independence. His revolt against the authority of his superiors in Spain resulted in independent friar provinces for the Philippines. His propagation of the dialects instead of Spanish – whatever his reasons for disobeying royal orders in this matter – bred an independent Philippine Christian culture that's not merely a mirror culture of the Spanish or the Mexican. He organised our dialects into grammars, opened up and mapped our lands, and pulled us out of the mists of folklore into the era of written history. The churches, roads, bridges, dams and irrigation systems he built, we are still using today. From any viewpoint, his is one of the great civilising labours in the history of mankind.

The typical Philippine town was structured more by the friars' Christianisation process than by Spain's civil officials. The stone church, with its massive baroque architecture, dwarfing bamboo and nipa houses, dominated the plaza and the *municipio* at the opposite end. In a landscape of coconut palm, it was a gigantic graphic of power. Through it, the friars were saying, 'We're in charge here now.'

The new town nucleus became a population centre, acting as a magnet to the scattered pre-colonial Filipino, who was enticed in and eventually adjusted himself 'under church bells' (*bajo los campanas*). Building churches and *convento*s with the aid of Chinese masons, the friar developed urban architecture, introducing new technology and materials for building. The rich ritual of the Spanish Church called for interior design, statuary, paintings and liturgical music. Out of these religious needs developed Philippine fine arts and practical arts and crafts, architecture, sculpture, a Western form of music and the theatre.

The friar exercised his revolutionary presence on the soil too. He introduced the wheel and the plough and harnessed the carabao (then only a source of meat) to them. He brought new crops from Spain, Mexico, Latin America and Spanish Africa, such as corn, tobacco, coffee, tea, cocoa, beans, onion, potato, guava, papaya, pineapple, avocado, squash, lettuce, cucumber, cabbage and peanuts, as well as new livestock like cows and horses. He charted the land, took the census, was inspector of schools and approved the fitness of candidates for the colonial army. The specifics of all this are on the records of the friar orders.

I'm going on about this because when I reached the Philippines in the seventies, the friar had been demonised. His massive contribution during the first two hundred years of colonisation had been erased in the public consciousness, and his less-than-glorious contribution during his remaining stint, when Spain's empire was collapsing, was superimposed on it. His positive influence was blotted out to the extent that, except for the Spanish churches here and there in Luzon and the Visayas, the friars might as well never have existed.

Except, of course, in the writings of one Jose Rizal.

Jose, Philippines' number-one patriot, but above all a propagandist for independence, made the friars the baddies in his two books, *Noli me Tangere* and *El Filibusterismo*. Few historians would disagree that he threw out the baby with the bathwater; political propagandists have no time for niceties. But the reputation he created stuck, became accepted as fact, and in a sense opened the way for me. With the friars gone, parishes priestless and churches in ruins, enter the new 'friar', the Columban, first to Manila and surrounding areas in 1929 and afterwards to Mindanao, Negros, Zambales and Pangasinan.

This appendix relies heavily on *Culture and History* (Solar Publishing, 1988), Nick Joaquin's collection of balanced and perceptive essays on Philippine history.

Glossary of Filipino words

allocutio	short sermon during a Legion of Mary meeting
amon	employer or boss
amorseko	a clinging type of hayseed
anito	a spirit in animist religion
bahala na	come what may
bahay kubo	nipa hut
bangka	outrigger canoe
banig	a mat woven from palm fronds
bayanihan	community in action
calamansi	lime juice
cogon	rough grass
convento	presbytery
dalaga	an unmarried lady
diwata	fairy in animist religion
haligil	wooden pillar
hiya	shame
ipilipil	a fast-growing small tree
kanya kanya	self-interest
mabait	kind, personable
Mahal na Araw	Holy Week
mestizo	Eurasian
Misa de Gallo	one of nine dawn Masses at Christmastime
municipio	the office of the mayor
ninang	godmother
ninong	godfather
pakikisama	good interpersonal relationship
palakasan	influence

palapala	a temporary shelter made of palm or bamboo
palikero	womaniser
pan de sal	small bread roll
purok	smallest unit of village or town
rondalla	native string band
sala	living room
sarisari	local store selling mixed goods
salubong	a meeting
santo	saint
tagapamagitan	intermediary
untang na loob	debt of gratitude

GLOSSARY OF IRISH WORDS

dúchas	innate nature or tradition
meitheal	community group in action
ráméis	loose, rubbishy talk
scéalaíocht	storytelling
tráithnín	dry grass stalk